LANDSCAPING
with TREES in
the MIDWEST

LANDSCAPING
with TREES in
the MIDWEST

A Guide for Residential
& Commercial Properties

Scott A. Zanon

OHIO UNIVERSITY PRESS

Athens

Ohio University Press, Athens, Ohio 45701
ohioswallow.com
© 2014 by Ohio University Press

To obtain permission to quote, reprint, or otherwise reproduce or distribute material
from Ohio University Press publications, please contact our rights and permissions
department at (740) 593-1154 or (740) 593-4536 (fax).

Printed in the United States of America
Ohio University Press books are printed on acid-free paper ∞ ™

24 23 22 21 20 19 18 17 16 15 14   5 4 3 2 1

Library of Congress Cataloging-in-Publication Data
Zanon, Scott A.
 Landscaping with trees in the Midwest : a guide for residential and commercial prop-
erties / Scott A. Zanon.
     pages cm
 Includes bibliographical references and index.
 ISBN 978-0-8040-1151-8 (pb : alk. paper) — ISBN 978-0-8040-4058-7 (pdf)
 1. Ornamental trees—Middle West. 2. Landscape design—Middle West. I. Title.
 SB435.52.M5Z37 2014
 635.9'7710977—dc23
                    2014007918

Contents

Foreword

to the First Edition

TREES ARE A beautiful and natural part of North American golf courses and landscapes, but in most cases they have either been taken for granted or neglected. The problem isn't that we as golfers don't put a high value on trees, for we often overvalue them. Rather, the problem is that we have not had good informational sources, specific to golf courses, to refer to and rely on for selecting and caring for golf course trees. Until now, that is.

Scott Zanon, author of this book, realized the lack of information on golf course trees when he served as chair of the Scarlet Golf Course Restoration Committee and as chair of the Green Committee for The Ohio State University golf courses—six holes on 300+ acres with lots of trees and tree issues. As is typical of most golf courses, there were few trees on the OSU property when the courses were built in the 1930s. Then, after World War II, seemingly everyone involved with the golf courses—including course superintendents, staff, coaches, green committees, golfers, and university officials—felt compelled to instigate planting more trees. By the 1990s, as many of the trees reached maturity, it became clear that they were either the wrong trees, were in the wrong place, or both, and, thereby, were adversely affecting the golf course and golfing experience. But a tree, once it reaches a certain size or stature, becomes somewhat sacred to a number of people who subsequently resist its removal, no matter what the negative consequences it causes or potential liability it poses. Scott, who has a Bachelor of Science degree in agriculture from OSU with majors in both agronomy (turfgrass science) and horticulture (landscape horticulture) took a more objective and balanced view of trees. However, when he proposed scientific reasons for tree renovations or removal, without golf-course-specific information sources he could use to convince folks what was the right thing to do, Scott faced stiff opposition. So he decided to write a user-friendly text to help others involved with trees in the home landscape and on larger properties such as golf courses.

The result is a book that doesn't just look good on the bookshelf. This book should become a well-used source of information to improve the health and beneficial qualities of trees.

In school we are taught that a "weed" is any plant out of its proper place: that includes trees. I have seen and experienced many instances where huge trees were simply "weeds" on the golf course. Perhaps the most dramatic example was a monstrous silver maple, with a girth of perhaps 80 to 90 inches, growing on the fourth tee at Scioto Country Club. The tree was not only degrading the turf on the tee through the normal negative influences of the shade that it produced, but its many surface roots were forcing the green's staff to hand water the tee more frequently in order to keep it uniformly green. Furthermore, the tree, as well as greatly complicating the daily maintenance of the tee, limited and reduced its effective size. The maple posed another problem—a threat of wrist injury to golfers taking a divot. In a more suitable location, this maple would have been revered; planted where it was, it was only loathed. Intellectually, almost everyone agreed the tree presented a significant problem that could only be solved by its removal, but they found it emotionally difficult to allow that to happen. But, happen it did, and now the tee and the entire golf hole are so dramatically improved that almost no one misses or even mentions that maple. Instead, they wonder why the tree wasn't taken out long ago.

So put Scott's knowledge to work for you. Use his experience, intellect, and insights to make your large or small property better.

Sincerely,

Michael J. Hurdzan, Ph.D.
ASGCA
Hurdzan Golf Design

Preface

to the Expanded Edition

IT HAS BEEN five years since the release of *Desirable Trees for the Midwest: 50 for the Home Landscape and Larger Properties*. I felt it was time to offer a somewhat different, expanded version with photographs, both new and a few old; 15 more trees to consider; and, of course, some new cultivars available in the trade.

In this edition, the vast majority of the color photographs are my own. From the many interactions I have had through book signings and speaking engagements, it is very evident that consumers greatly appreciate seeing the trees in their various forms throughout the growing seasons. Why pay a large amount of money for a tree without knowing or being able to see what it looks like in progressing stages of the year? I took the photographs using a Panasonic Lumix digital camera along with an Apple iPhone.

There are 15 more trees recommended in this edition for the Midwest. Because of the warmer temperature shifts in our climate, more trees were added. These trees still are site specific, each requiring its particular shade, protection, and/or watering needs.

That people from homeowners to green industry professionals actually use the book as a reference has been very rewarding to me. Whether a tree is selected to be grown for shade, fall color, ornamental bark, or spring flowering, or for another purpose, this book will give you the ability to visualize the tree and read about its culture before it is planted. Gone are the days of only looking at illustrations and/or black and white photographs.

From a "green" perspective, trees are a very important part of the environment, one that helps to beautify communities and neighborhoods. A well-designed landscape not only can add beauty to your property but also can reduce your cooling and heating costs. Carefully positioned trees can save up to 25 percent of the energy a typical household uses. Research shows that summer daytime air temperatures can be three to six degrees cooler in tree-shaded neighborhoods than in treeless areas.

Trees can help a home be more energy efficient by providing shade, reflecting heat, and blocking those cold winter winds. Deciduous shade trees planted to the south and west will help keep your home cool in the summer and allow sun to shine through the windows in the winter. They also cool sidewalks and driveways that reflect heat. Planting evergreen trees to the north and west can block winter winds, improving energy efficiency.

The emerald ash borer continues to wreak its havoc across the Midwestern parts of the United States. The effects are devastating. This book offers solid replacement alternatives for those unfortunate enough to lose an ash tree.

This edition is published in a very nice compact 7 x 10-inch paperback form. Compared to the first edition, costs have been decreased, enabling, I hope, more readers to get this book into their hands.

Thank you for your ongoing support and enthusiasm.

Preface
to the First Edition

WHEN I WAS asked to chair the Scarlet Restoration Committee at The Ohio State University Golf Club in 2003 by Director of Athletics Andy Geiger, little did I know that it would lead me to write this book.

We removed quite a few trees from the Scarlet Golf Course and I quickly realized there were no guides or writings listing desirable trees for use on golf courses. Naturally, this crosses over into many other areas, too.

With so many golf courses now taking out larger amounts of overgrown, poorly selected, and site-planted trees, it made sense that they have a replanting program established with the idea to plant trees more suitable to the golf course but more importantly for the growth of turfgrass.

I have tried very hard to make this user-friendly to all readers whether they are golf course superintendents, golf course architects, green committee members, horticulturists, arborists, grounds professionals, master gardeners, home gardeners, or homeowners.

Cultivars are listed but are not necessarily functionally better than the species. Cultivars are normally selected for marketing characteristics or purposes.

I sincerely hope this book is informative, useful, and educational for all of you. I also hope it provides thought and reason for help in selecting the desirable tree.

For additional copies of this book, please visit www.desirabletrees.com.

Acknowledgments

THIS BOOK WOULD not be possible without the support and assistance of many special friends and people. It was a long journey—one that took longer than anticipated—but nonetheless was very rewarding. Writing a book takes discipline and requires much patience.

I wish to thank Ohio State University Professor Emeritus Dr. Steven Still for his advice, guidance, and photographs. I was privileged to have Steven, a true plantsman, as my instructor and mentor for all of my OSU horticulture identification classes, consisting of woody plants, trees, shrubs, and perennials. He is currently Executive Director of the Perennial Plant Association.

I wish to thank Dr. Michael Hurdzan, ASGCA, for his encouragement to author this book. A noted and respected golf course architect, Mike has received the Donald Ross Award from the American Society of Golf Course Architects. This award is given annually to a person who has made significant contributions to the game of golf and golf course architecture. It is the organization's highest honor.

I wish to thank OSU Professor Dr. Karl Danneberger who thought I had a good idea that would be helpful when I approached him about writing this book. An agronomist, Karl is a noted turfgrass expert in the Department of Horticulture and Crop Science.

The following individuals and organizations helped in numerous ways—from providing photographs and literature, sharing their knowledge and experience, and allowing me to ask their advice. They are:

James Chatfield: Associate Professor and Extension Specialist, Department of Horticulture and Crop Science and Department of Plant Pathology; The Ohio State University

Steve Cothrel: Superintendent of Parks & Forestry; City of Upper Arlington, Ohio

Dr. David Gardner: Associate Professor, Department of Horticulture and Crop Science; The Ohio State University

Dr. Randall Heiligmann: Professor Emeritus, School of Environment and Natural Resources; The Ohio State University

Doug Knaup: Horticulturist; The Ohio State University Golf Club

Robin Knaup: Willoway Nurseries, Inc.

Mark Kroggel: Research Specialist, The School of Plant Sciences; University of Arizona

Dr. T. Davis Sydnor: Professor Emeritus in Urban Forestry, School of Environment and Natural Resources; The Ohio State University

HAIKU

With spring's emergence
Blooms dazzle and scents abound
Baring gardeners' souls

Summer's hot and dry
Days are long and bountiful
Sunrise to sunset

Fall is the season
When the autumnal leaves drop
Gently to earth's floor

The long winter nights
Allow nature's plants to rest
'Til the thaws commence

—Author

Trees versus Turf

(an ongoing problem)

S HOULD ONE PLANT trees or turf? This age-old battle continues to be waged. Trees and grasses do not *naturally* coexist. Grasses do not grow in the forests and trees do not flourish in the prairies. However, with some common sense and knowledge, they can *peacefully* coexist.

Although trees and turfgrass are both effective landscape plants, each has different needs concerning growing conditions, light and nutrition requirements, and moisture levels. Problems occur when the care of trees and turf are not separated. Management requirements of each tend to compromise the other. But, ecological tree removal often clashes with political and emotional issues. People in general do not like to cut down trees.

Property owners across the country are beginning to pay attention to the turfgrass they so lovingly care for. One of the main culprits of poor turf growth is too much shade. Consequently many larger, older trees are being thinned, limbed-up, or simply removed.

Shade causes poor turfgrass performance beneath trees by reducing turf quality and quantity. Grass growing under a shade tree is usually weak, thin, and subject to weed invasion for several reasons. Light quality is the crucial issue. The green tree leaves filter the critical light wavelengths for photosynthesis. As a consequence, turfgrass receives a smaller quantity and a poorer quality of light.

Shade creates other major stress factors. Reduced airflow and increased humidity levels may contribute to disease issues. An increase of air movement usually results in a decrease of diseases. Tree roots compete with grass for both water and nutrients. While this root competition can promote stress, lack of light remains the primary problem.

Morning shade has a great negative impact on turfgrass. Trees on the east and southeast sides of properties create this morning shade. Grass planted in these areas does not receive the benefit of early morning sunlight and, additionally, dew does not evaporate quickly, thus extending cooler leaf and soil temperatures. Eliminate the morning shade issue by limbing-up, thinning, or by removing the entire tree. Trees that block morning sunlight must be considered for removal as morning sun is more valuable than afternoon sun, So take heed.

Despite their differences, turf and trees can peacefully coexist and even thrive together. Achieving that balance can be attained. Armed with an understanding of how each affects the other, decisions can be reached regarding methods to modify the environment and maintenance procedures that will optimize the growing conditions for both. But good planning and proper tree selection are crucial.

Why Plant Trees?

GREAT QUESTION, isn't it? It is difficult to grow grass under them; they are the recipient of most of the water and sunlight; their branching obstructs natural lines of sight and play. Yet, with all of these problems, the mere mention or sound of a chainsaw elicits trepidation and panic. Most human beings are tree-huggers by nature; we tend to become emotionally attached to our trees.

Imagine a park, street, or yard without a tree. What a lonely expanse of nothingness that would be. Trees are integral components of landscapes. They add grace and inspiration as well as architectural beauty. Trees have a practical side, too: they can help a home be more energy efficient by providing shade, reflecting heat, and blocking cold winter winds.

While problems tend to surface with mature trees, all trees have their good and bad points. It is rare to find a tree that will make its owner happy over its lifespan. But today, caretakers of public properties and homeowners have the option to make decisions and actions about removing trees when they want. For far too long, we gave little financial or planning consideration to trees. But when tree plantings overshadow the care of turfgrass, a slow, downward, agronomic spiral begins.

With so many trees now being removed because of structural issues, diseases, or insect infestations, or just by choice, the ability and opportunity to replant a property is afforded. Better consideration can be used when locating the trees and in selecting more suitable trees, ones that will help in the growth of turfgrass and beautify the property.

Reducing competition among trees and selecting more desirable specimens or functional trees is a wonderful gift for others to appreciate in the future. But there are many reasons for planting trees; it is important to have a specific purpose in mind. Overplanting is a costly error that affects future budgets. Focus on quality, not quantity.

Since trees are a major element of North American landscapes, we must learn more about their care, form, and function. It is also imperative to maintain tree species diversity in case of catastrophic diseases, like Dutch elm disease, or infestations of insects, such as the emerald ash borer.

Climate change is occurring due to daily human activities that emit exorbitant quantities of greenhouse gases (carbon dioxide emissions) into the global atmosphere. Trees are a tremendous biological means of sequestering carbon (CO^2), thereby helping to offset fossil fuel emissions. They store carbon and are known as nature's "carbon sinks." So planting trees helps the environment, too.

When planting a tree, enjoy its present but cherish it in its posterity. A tree can quickly outgrow its original purpose or it can slowly grow into its intended one.

Selecting Trees

WHEN SELECTING TREES to plant, moderation and common sense have to meet. Choose varieties that will not negatively impact property lines and power lines when fully mature. Very simply: do the math. Find out what the tree's mature size (height and width) will be and work backwards. Remember not to plant on the east or southeast sites where shade from the tree will ultimately cause problems. Before digging, be sure to contact your local utility company to mark gas lines, water pipes, or underground cables. The wrong tree species in the wrong location is a recipe for disaster. Future tree removal is problematic and expensive.

When purchasing new trees, disregard the end-of-the-season closeout offerings from local nurseries. There usually is a reason no one else purchased these leftover trees: a poor condition, a deformed shape, an ultra-common type, or a species not hardy to the area. Making that extra effort to purchase and plant high-quality, desirable trees for a location will benefit all involved immensely. Select the tree based on your criteria and use the plant usage guides in this book to recommend viable options for you.

Form and habit should be considered before making a decision for your property or garden. Architectural structure is important, especially during the winter months. Trees exhibiting an interesting shape or outline may still be appreciated when other plants are either dormant or dead. They may have weeping, arching, or sculpted branching. They may have dramatic or rounded canopies. They may be vase-shaped, pyramidal, or cascading. The appealing characteristic simply may be the massive trunk of the tree.

When selecting a tree to plant, habit is a wonderful characteristic to consider before making a decision. It is great to have all of the ornamental features, but a tree with appealing form and structure is appreciated throughout all four seasons; such a tree usually improves with age.

When properly selected, planted, and maintained, trees can add a needed dimension architecturally. Great properties and gardens have reputations for their tree plantings. But, comprehensive programs designed to care for existing trees and to plan properly for new plantings as they become necessary are vital.

Selective Pruning
and Shade Seeding

Varying amounts of tree work are ongoing on practically every property, yet the removal and pruning of trees remains an emotional issue. Therefore, to avoid the inevitable backlash such emotions raise, the best time to do selective pruning or tree removal is in the winter or, for public grounds, during off-season.

Selective pruning, when care is taken not to ruin the shape of a tree or a shrub, will allow most trees to remain on-site and help to allow enough sunlight to filter through canopies for good turfgrass growth. Selective pruning also increases air circulation, thereby generally decreasing excess humidity and disease problems.

Selective thinning will allow some light through. A great rule of thumb is to remove no more than one-quarter of a tree's foliage crown in a single pruning. Limbing-up of trees or raising the canopy of trees that branch to the ground has proven to be a very effective method of pruning without affecting the beauty of the surrounding landscape. In fact, it usually enhances views. This procedure prunes lower limbs back to the trunk, thus increasing airflow and decreasing shade.

Ultimately, however, one cannot prune enough to solve a serious shade issue. Some trees just need to be removed. In these cases, the problem is light quality, *not* light quantity. Most courses and properties that remove trees for the benefits of increased air circulation and sunlight will likely end up with some pretty great views, too. Removing trees alleviates the problems; the best way to *avoid* those problems is thoughtful planning. Watch where you plant your trees.

Morning light is critical for turfgrass. Avoid planting trees on the east and south sides of properties and in important turf locations like front- or backyards; planted there, trees will block the crucial morning sun so vital for optimum turfgrass growth. As increased sunlight helps turfgrass become hardier, healthier, and less prone to disease, the necessity for applications of fungicides, insecticides, and fertilizer will be reduced.

When planting turf in shaded areas, consider the needs of the grasses you choose. Fine-leaf fescues are considered the most shade tolerant of the cool-season grasses. They include creeping red fescue and chewings fescue. Turf-type tall fescue does well in moderate shade.

Fall seeding in shaded areas is preferred. The turf tends to be more successful as it enters the summer months due to better root systems and larger stored-food reserves.

Late fall fertilization of cool-season grasses is very beneficial in shaded environments. Late fall really is the only time of the year when grass beneath the trees can effectively utilize the nitrogen without tree competition for nutrients, light, and moisture. During spring and summer, trees with shallow fibrous root systems compete fiercely with turfgrass for moisture.

If all else fails, then the planting of shade-tolerant ground covers in heavily shaded areas is suggested. They look and work great.

Tree Cultural Practices

Planting

THERE ARE TWO ideal *times* to plant trees: fall is the best season; early spring is a good alternative time. However, planting the correct *way* can make the difference as to whether a plant survives its crucial first year. How the plant is packaged influences the condition of its roots; that, in turn, determines how to put the tree in the ground to thrive.

There are three types of plant packaging: bare-root, container-grown, and balled-and-burlapped (B&B).

Bare Root

Most mail-order catalogs ship purchased plants in bare-root form. These are harvested from fields with no soil attached to the roots. These plants are very perishable and should be both purchased and planted prior to spring budbreak. The advantage of bare-root plants is that they allow a thorough inspection of the root system prior to planting.

After taking possession of the plant, one must keep a bare-root plant damp, being careful not to allow its roots to dry out prior to planting. Even though it is in a dormant state, the plant is alive and requires water to survive. Keep it out of direct sunlight, too.

Prior to planting, carefully inspect and prune the roots. With pruners, re-move all damaged and/or turned-in roots. Keep your pruning blades sharp: clean cuts heal faster and decrease the chances of disease.

Dig a hole wide enough to allow roots to spread into their natural position. It must also be deep enough so the crown of the tree will be at or just above the soil line. Break up any soil clods to prevent air pockets and backfill half of the

9

hole. Slowly water to settle the soil around the roots. Continue to backfill the hole, then water again to settle the remainder of the soil. At this point, many people use their feet to tamp the soil. All that really does is promote compaction; it should be avoided. Be sure to keep the soil around these plants moist as bare-root plants will initially require more frequent watering than those container-grown or balled-and-burlapped.

Container Grown

The most popular option for consumers is container-grown plants. These plants are grown above the ground in a pot, filled not with real soil but with an artificial medium, leading to much easier handling.

Regardless of the material, remove and discard the container prior to planting. Inspect the roots. Gently loosen (but do not remove) the whitish-colored roots from the surface of the soil ball. This allows expansion of the roots into the new soil site and is imperative for the tree's survival.

Again using sharp pruners, cut out the woody, thick roots to prevent them girdling the trunk. The flow of water and food is greatly decreased throughout the plant if girdling occurs. If the plant is root bound, use a sharp knife to slice it from top to bottom in three to four spots, being careful to make the cuts two to three inches deep. In a healthy plant, new roots will sprout from these cuts.

Dig a hole two to three times wider than the width of the container; this allows emerging roots to expand horizontally into the loose soil. Allow the crown of the tree to be slightly above grade level. Set the plant, backfill halfway, then water to settle the soil. Finish backfilling and water again to settle the rest of the soil. Do not tamp the soil as it will promote compaction.

B&B

Larger trees and shrubs typically are sold balled and burlapped (B&B). B&B plants are field dug, with a ball of soil wrapped in burlap surrounding the roots. These plants are mainly available at nurseries as their weight makes them difficult to ship and cumbersome to work with. That being said, larger plants are often only available in this form.

Dig a hole two to three times wider than the root ball; this allows emerging roots to expand horizontally into the loose soil near the soil surface where more oxygen is present. Make sure the root-ball top sits just above the soil grade.

After the plant is placed properly in the hole, backfill halfway and water to reduce air pocket development. This will also assist in stabilizing the plant. Contrary to popular belief, remove all wire or rope tied around the main trunk and remove the burlap from the top of the root ball. The burlap on the bottom of the root ball will decompose and disintegrate as the roots grow through it and expand.

Backfill and attempt to break up large clods of soil preventing air pockets. Construct a raised berm around the outside planting hole. Do not place extra soil on top of the root ball. Gently water inside of the berm allowing the soil to settle around the root ball. Once again, do not use your feet to tamp the area.

Watering

One inch of water per week during the first year is a good guide. In our northern climate, irrigate until the ground freezes. During dry periods, water established trees every 10 to 14 days.

Mycorrhizal Fungi

This soil treatment (supplement) for trees is a standard part of reforestry practices in most areas of the world and has been around since the 1850s. Coexisting with trees and plants in nature, these beneficial fungi provide a safety net for the tree in times of stress. By colonizing the roots and extending themselves further into the soil, the fungi enable the tree to absorb more nutrients and moisture, resulting in a healthier tree better capable of tolerating stressful conditions.

Fertilizing

New plantings should not be fertilized during the first year. For established plants, in the early spring use a complete fertilizer at a rate of two pounds per one inch of trunk diameter. Apply a second application at the same rate in late summer. An easy and effective way to apply the granular fertilizer is with a broadcast spreader.

Mulching

A layer of mulch, three to four inches deep, around newly planted or established trees helps maintain soil moisture, smothers weeds, regulates temperature, and protects from the dreaded trimmer or lawnmower trunk damage (lawn mower blight).

Pruning

Inspect your new planting and remove any broken, dead, or diseased limbs. Wait one to two years before beginning to train and shape. Use selective pruning for established trees as needed to maintain size, shape, and to encourage growth, flowering, and fruiting. Most plants respond favorably to late winter or early spring pruning. It is also easier to see what needs to be pruned when leaves are absent. Remember, though, to prune spring-blooming plants right after they flower, not before, or no flowers will exist.

Staking

Proper staking is done to prevent the root ball from rocking; it is not intended to prevent the top of the tree from being blown about by the wind. A stable root ball is necessary for good root development. But almost all staking should be removed after one year; many times staking is not even warranted.

List of 65 Desirable Trees

Deciduous Trees

1. *Acer buergerianum*—Trident Maple
2. *Acer griseum*—Paperbark Maple
3. *Acer pensylvanicum*—Striped Maple; Moosewood; Snake Bark Maple
4. *Acer rubrum* Red Maple; Swamp Maple
5. *Acer saccharum*—Sugar Maple; Rock Maple; Hard Maple
6. *Aesculus octandra*—Yellow Buckeye
7. *Aesculus parviflora*—Bottlebrush Buckeye
8. *Aesculus pavia*—Red Buckeye
9. *Amelanchier* spp.—Serviceberry; Juneberry; Sarvisberry; Saskatoon; Shadblow; Shadbush
10. *Asimina triloba*—Common Pawpaw; Custard Apple
11. *Betula nigra*—River Birch
12. *Carpinus betulus*—European Hornbeam; Common Hornbeam
13. *Carpinus caroliniana*—American Hornbeam; Musclewood; Blue Beech; Ironwood
14. *Cercidiphyllum japonicum*—Katsuratree
15. *Cercis canadensis*—Eastern Redbud
16. *Chionanthus virginicus*—White Fringetree
17. *Cladrastis kentukea*—American Yellowwood
18. *Cornus alternifolia*—Pagoda Dogwood; Alternate-leaf Dogwood
19. *Cornus florida*—Flowering Dogwood
20. *Cornus kousa*—Kousa Dogwood; Chinese Dogwood

21. *Cornus mas*—Corneliancherry Dogwood

22. *Fagus sylvatica*—European Beech

23. *Franklinia alatamaha*—Franklinia; Franklin Tree

24. *Ginkgo biloba*—Ginkgo; Maidenhair Tree

25. *Gleditsia triacanthos* var. *inermis*—Thornless Honeylocust

26. *Gymnocladus dioicus*—Kentucky Coffeetree

27. *Halesia carolina*—Carolina Silverbell

28. *Heptacodium miconioides*—Seven-son Flower

29. *Koelreuteria paniculata*—Panicled Goldenraintree; Varnish Tree

30. *Liriodendron tulipifera*—Tuliptree; Tulip Poplar; Yellow Poplar

31. *Magnolia acuminata*—Cucumbertree Magnolia; Cucumber Magnolia

32. *Magnolia stellata*—Star Magnolia

33. *Magnolia virginiana*—Sweetbay Magnolia; Laurel Magnolia

34. *Malus* spp.—Flowering Crabapple

35. *Nyssa sylvatica*—Black Tupelo; Black Gum; Sour Gum

36. *Ostrya virginiana*—American Hophornbeam; Ironwood

37. *Oxydendrum arboreum*—Sourwood; Lily of the Valley Tree; Sorrel Tree

38. *Parrotia persica*—Persian Parrotia; Persian Ironwood

39. *Quercus acutissima*—Sawtooth Oak

40. *Quercus bicolor*—Swamp White Oak

41. *Quercus imbricaria*—Shingle Oak; Laurel Oak

42. *Quercus muehlenbergii*—Chinkapin Oak; Yellow Chestnut Oak

43. *Quercus palustris*—Pin Oak

44. *Quercus rubra*—Red Oak; Eastern Red Oak; Northern Red Oak

45. *Quercus shumardii*—Shumard Oak

46. *Sassafras albidum*—Common Sassafras

47. *Stewartia pseudocamellia*—Japanese Stewartia

48. *Styrax japonicus*—Japanese Snowbell

49. *Syringa pekinensis*—Pekin Lilac; Chinese Tree Lilac; Peking Lilac

50. *Syringa reticulata*—Japanese Tree Lilac

51. *Tilia cordata*—Littleleaf Linden

52. *Tilia tomentosa*—Silver Linden

53. *Ulmus americana*—American Elm (resistant cultivars)

54. *Ulmus parviflora*—Lacebark Elm; Chinese Elm

55. *Ulmus* x *Frontier*—Frontier Elm

56. *Zelkova serrata*—Japanese Zelkova

Coniferous Trees

1. *Abies balsamea* var. *phanerolepis*—Canaan Fir

2. *Abies concolor*—White Fir; Concolor Fir

3. *Juniperus virginiana*—Eastern Redcedar

4. *Metasequoia glyptostroboides*—Dawn Redwood (deciduous)

5. *Picea omorika*—Serbian Spruce

6. *Picea orientalis*—Oriental Spruce

7. *Pinus bungeana*—Lacebark Pine

8. *Pinus strobus*—Eastern White Pine

9. *Taxodium distichum*—Common Baldcypress (deciduous)

Tree Growth Rates
& Sizes Table

Growth

Slow: < 12' yearly

Medium: 12–24' yearly

Fast: > 24' yearly

Size

Small: < 30'

Medium: 30–50'

Large: > 50'

United States Hardiness
Zone Maps

(pages 18–19)

arborday.org Hardiness Zones Map

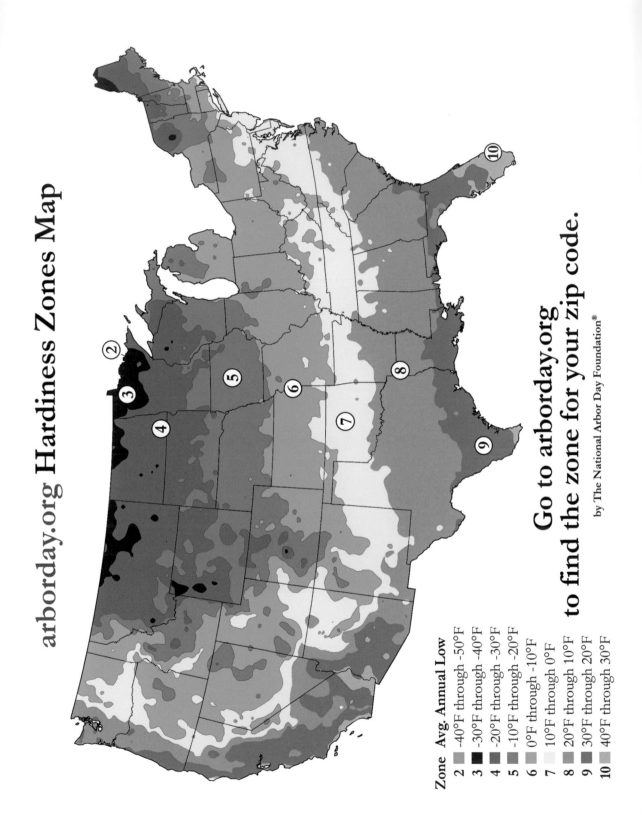

Go to arborday.org
to find the zone for your zip code.

by The National Arbor Day Foundation®

Zone Avg. Annual Low
2 -40°F through -50°F
3 -30°F through -40°F
4 -20°F through -30°F
5 -10°F through -20°F
6 0°F through -10°F
7 10°F through 0°F
8 20°F through 10°F
9 30°F through 20°F
10 40°F through 30°F

Arborday.org Hardiness Zones
Alaska and Hawaii

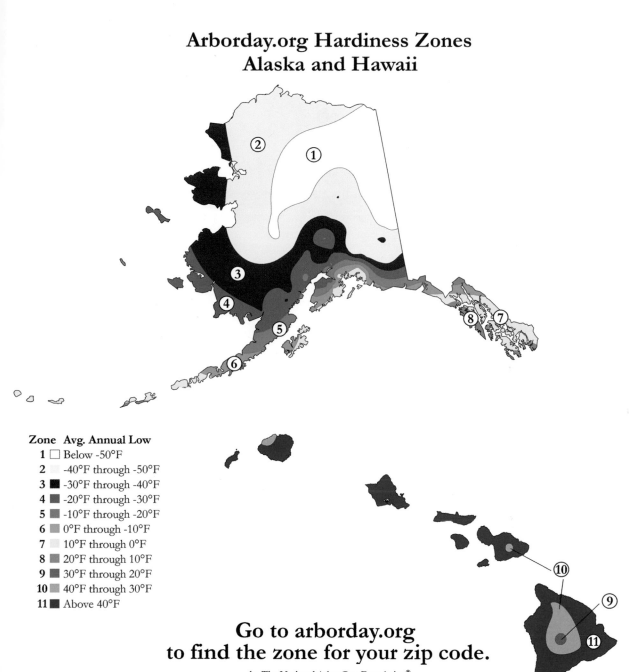

Zone	Avg. Annual Low
1	Below -50°F
2	-40°F through -50°F
3	-30°F through -40°F
4	-20°F through -30°F
5	-10°F through -20°F
6	0°F through -10°F
7	10°F through 0°F
8	20°F through 10°F
9	30°F through 20°F
10	40°F through 30°F
11	Above 40°F

Go to arborday.org
to find the zone for your zip code.

by The National Arbor Day Foundation®

Individual List
by Scientific Name
with Color Photographs

Scientific Name: *Acer buergerianum*

Common Name: Trident Maple

Hardiness Zones: 5–9

Mature Size: 20–30' tall x wide

Habit: Oval–rounded

Growth Rate: Slow

Bark: Gray–brown–orange; exfoliating with age; good winter interest

Leaf Color: Glossy, dark green

Fall Color: Yellow–orange–red, but late and at times variable

Flowers: Green–yellow in April, but inconspicuous

Fruit: Samara

Disease & Insect Problems: None serious

Culture: Prefers well-drained acid soil; full sun; displays good drought resistance

Recommended Cultivar:
  'ABMTF' (Aeryn®): clonal selection providing less variability; medium–fast grower; excellent fall color; great street-tree potential

Author Notes: This single-trunked, small shade tree is a handsome addition to any area and is underutilized. The three-lobed leaf is unusual as it looks like a duck's foot. In certain years the tree can produce a heavy fruit-set of samaras which could clutter annual or perennial beds and present problems of germination later. Sometimes the Trident Maple is difficult to source but it is worth the effort.

Scientific Name: *Acer griseum*

Common Name: Paperbark Maple

Hardiness Zones: 4–8

Mature Size: 20–30' tall x 15' wide

Habit: Upright oval

Growth Rate: Slow

Bark: Peeling cinnamon; exfoliating; visually striking

Leaf Color: Dark blue–green trifoliate leaf

Fall Color: Bronze–red late; often October and November

Flowers: Green in May, but not ornamental

Fruit: Samara

Disease & Insect Problems: None serious

Culture: Prefers well-drained, moist, acid soil; adaptable to clay soil; full sun to partial shade

Recommended Cultivars: None

Author Notes: A true specimen, this small ornamental tree has unrivaled aesthetic qualities. It is somewhat expensive but worth the splendor of its year-round appeal. Have patience for its slow growth as the reward is outstanding. The Paperbark Maple is a four-season plant.

Scientific Name: *Acer pensylvanicum*

Common Names: Striped Maple
Moosewood
Snake Bark Maple

Hardiness Zones: 3–7

Mature Size: 15–25' tall & wide

Habit: Upright and sometimes multi-stemmed

Growth Rate: Slow

Bark: Young branches >½" are green with conspicuous long, vertical, white stripes; stripes are absent on mature trunks

Leaf Color: Bright green

Fall Color: Brilliant clear yellow to golden

Flowers: Yellow to yellow–green in May; produced on slender pendulous racemes

Fruit: Samara

Disease & Insect Problems: The most serious is Verticillium wilt

Culture: Prefers partial or light shade and cool, moist, well-drained, slightly acidic soil; not tolerant of poor soils, heat, or drought

Recommended Cultivars:
'Erythrocladum': bark of twigs have a beautiful bright coral–red winter color
'White Tigress': green bark with pronounced white striations; more heat tolerant

Author Notes: A lovely small tree that should be pruned as needed to show off its beautiful bark. Typical of an understory tree, the Striped Maple is not tolerant of afternoon sun. In order to flourish it needs proper cultural conditions to be considered. The bark and fall color are very worthy. Plant it where one can enjoy its beauty during the winter months.

Scientific Name: *Acer rubrum*

Common Names: Red Maple
Swamp Maple

Hardiness Zones: 3–9

Mature Size: 70' tall x 40' wide; 'Cultivars' smaller

Habit: Pyramidal to elliptical

Growth Rate: Medium–fast

Bark: Soft gray to gray–brown

Leaf Color: Emerging red-tinged, then becoming medium–dark green

Fall Color: Green–yellow to yellow to red; 'Cultivars' best for fall color

Flowers: Red and noticeable before foliage; March–April

Fruit: Samara

Disease & Insect Problems: Leaf scorch and Verticillium wilt, but not common

Culture: Tolerant of many soils and pH levels; will tolerate wet soil; full to partial sun; shows manganese deficiency (chlorosis) in high pH soil

Recommended Cultivars:
'Autumn Flame': smaller leaf; red fall color two weeks earlier than species
'Autumn Radiance': glowing fall color two weeks early; 'October Glory' x 'Red Sunset'
'Autumn Spire': columnar; scarlet fall color; very hardy
'Bowhall': upright and pyramidal but wider; yellow–orange–red fall color
'Columnare': upright and tolerant of dry summer conditions
'Franksred' (Red Sunset®): upright; outstanding orange–red fall color
'October Glory': rounded; crimson fall color develops later than others
'Red Rocket': upright; cold hardy; intense red fall color
'Sun Valley': long lasting orange–red fall color; 'Red Sunset' x 'Autumn Flame'

Author Notes: Straight species is a large shade tree. 'Cultivars' would be considered a medium common shade and autumn accent tree and are preferred. The Red Maple is an excellent specimen tree and is valued for its relatively quick growth, good shade, and elegant symmetry in youth. Surface roots can be a concern.

Scientific Name: *Acer saccharum*

Common Names: Sugar Maple
Hard Maple
Rock Maple

Hardiness Zones: 3–8

Mature Size: 60–80' tall x 40' wide

Habit: Upright oval to rounded

Growth Rate: Medium

Bark: Smooth gray–brown becoming furrowed with age; irregular plates

Leaf Color: Medium–dark green

Fall Color: Yellow–orange–red and striking

Flowers: Green–yellow in April but not showy

Fruit: Samara

Disease & Insect Problems: Leaf scorch in droughty conditions; Verticillium wilt

Culture: Prefers well-drained, moist, fertile soil; full sun; very adaptable to pH
levels; can be difficult to establish; frost-cracking sometimes a problem

Recommended Cultivars:
'Adirondack': pyramidal; golden orange fall color two weeks earlier than species
'Bailsta' (Fall Fiesta™): very cold hardy; fall color is outstanding with far more
oranges and reds than other sugar maples
'Commemoration': deep yellow–orange–red fall color two weeks earlier than species
'Goldspire': columnar; bright yellow–orange fall color
'Green Mountain': fast grower with cold and heat tolerance; yellow–orange fall color
'Legacy': fast grower with excellent heat tolerance; yellow to orange–red fall color
'Wright Brothers': fast grower; fall color tends to be more red

Author Notes: This stately, large shade tree is one of the best. It may be used as a
specimen or autumn accent tree and is a landscape standout. Some cultivars are
available for excellent fall color. Overall, the Sugar Maple is generally thought of
as a poor urban selection but its fall color is often spectacular.

Scientific Name: *Aesculus octandra (flava)*

Common Name: Yellow Buckeye

Hardiness Zones: 4–8

Mature Size: 60–75' tall x 40' wide

Habit: Upright oval

Growth Rate: Medium

Bark: Gray–brown with large, flat, smooth plates

Leaf Color: Dark green

Fall Color: Pumpkin orange to yellow–brown

Flowers: Yellow inflorescence in mid-May

Fruit: Smooth pear-shaped capsule splitting in October to yield two brown nuts

Disease & Insect Problems: None serious

Culture: Prefers deep, moist, well-drained soil along with full to partial shade

Recommended Cultivars: None

Author Notes: This stately, handsome, large shade tree is preferable to *A. glabra* (Ohio Buckeye) because it is less susceptible to leaf scorch. With its attractive dark green palmate leaf changing to beautiful pumpkin fall foliage, the Yellow Buckeye is considered to be the best large buckeye tree.

Scientific Name: *Aesculus parviflora*

Common Name: Bottlebrush Buckeye

Hardiness Zones: 4–8

Mature Size: 10' tall & wide

Habit: Wide-spreading, multi-stemmed mound

Growth Rate: Slow, but suckers (basal) grow quickly and require pruning

Bark: Ash gray

Leaf Color: Dark green and drooping form

Fall Color: Yellow–green to yellow–brown to clear yellow which can be outstanding

Flowers: White extending 1" beyond petals (bottlebrush-like) in July; usually a stunning two-week show on 10" long x 3" wide inflorescences

Fruit: Light brown smooth capsule

Disease & Insect Problems: None serious

Culture: Prefers well-drained moist soil; pH adaptable; full sun to partial shade

Recommended Cultivars:
 'Rogers': blooms later and has more flowers which tend to slightly droop

Author Notes: This sprawling, multi-stemmed, medium shrub/small tree is excellent for massing, border, or specimen and can be used under shade trees or shade beds. This is a superb understory plant that is finally becoming more recognized and available.

Scientific Name: *Aesculus pavia*

Common Name: Red Buckeye

Hardiness Zones: 4–8

Mature Size: 10–20' tall & wide

Habit: Rounded

Growth Rate: Slow–medium

Bark: Light brown and smooth in youth becoming flaky and attractive with age

Leaf Color: Dark green

Fall Color: Yellow–brown; early drop in late September

Flowers: Showy red 6" panicles in May; attract hummingbirds

Fruit: Smooth, round, tan capsules

Disease & Insect Problems: Some leaf scorch in hot, dry summers possible

Culture: Ideally suited in partial shade to full sun; prefers moist, well-drained soil

Recommended Cultivars: None

Author Notes: This handsome, small ornamental tree in flower makes a fine specimen. Since it does drop its leaves early, place it around other plants and let its branches provide a coarse architectural interest. The Red Buckeye is found as single- or multi-trunked forms.

Scientific Name: *Amelanchier species*

Common Names: Serviceberry
Juneberry
Sarvisberry
Saskatoon
Shadblow
Shadbush

Hardiness Zones: 4–9

Mature Size: 6–30' tall x 4–10' wide; 'Cultivars', 12' tall x 10' wide

Habit: Upright oval

Growth Rate: Slow–medium

Bark: Gray and smooth; striped when older; ornamental feature

Leaf Color: Medium green

Fall Color: Yellow to orange to red in October, often in spectacular fashion

Flowers: Showy white in mid-April

Fruit: Purple–black at maturity and edible (sweet); ripens in June; robins and squirrels often devour the fruit; Species is a commercial fruit tree in Canada

Disease & Insect Problems: None serious

Culture: Prefers moist, rich, well-drained soils; full sun to partial shade; very adaptable

Recommended Cultivars:
Amelanchier alnifolia (Saskatoon Serviceberry) 'Regent': mounding compact type
Amelanchier canadensis (Shadblow Serviceberry) 'Glennform' (Rainbow Pillar®): upright columnar habit suggesting use as screen or hedge
Amelanchier x *grandiflora* (Apple Serviceberry) is a hybrid of *A. arborea* (Downy Serviceberry) and *A. laevis* 'Autumn Brilliance': profuse flowering and bright red fall color that fades to orange
Amelanchier laevis (Cumulus Serviceberry) 'Cumulus': vigorous upright growth habit with orange–red fall color; good street tree
Amelanchier laevis lamarckii (Allegheny Serviceberry) 'Lamarckii': cultivar that is somewhat smaller and has an upright growth habit

Author Notes: This is one of the best four-season, small-to-medium, ornamental trees that is available either multi- or single-trunked. It functions well in a naturalistic setting or as a specimen. There are many species and cultivars to choose from. Author is known to make a very tasty Serviceberry pie and prefers *A. laevis* for sentimental reasons.

Scientific Name: *Asimina triloba*

Common Names: Common Pawpaw
Custard Apple

Hardiness Zones: 5–9

Mature Size: 15–20' tall & wide

Habit: Conical and narrow; typically as a multi-stemmed tree or shrub

Growth Rate: Slow–medium

Bark: Dark brown–gray in youth; scaly and rough when older

Leaf Color: Medium–dark green

Fall Color: Yellow

Flowers: Maroon–dark purple typically in May

Fruit: Green–yellow edible berry of many shapes (rounded–oblong–elongated); ripe when brown with the soft orange flesh having a consistency of custard and flavors of banana and pear; animals tend to relish the fruits

Disease & Insect Problems: None serious

Culture: Full sun or shade and best in moist, fertile, deep, slightly acid, well-drained soils

Recommended Cultivars: None

Author Notes: This small tree has the largest edible fruit native to North America. The Pawpaw is native to shady, rich bottomlands, where it often forms dense undergrowth (thicket) in the forest as it tends to produce root-suckers a few feet from the trunk. It is a native understory tree that needs regular watering during the growing season and does not tolerate heavy, wet, alkaline soils. This plant is a candidate to be used more often in the landscape, perhaps for naturalizing areas. I have also seen it used as a street tree.

Scientific Name: *Betula nigra*

Common Name: River Birch

Hardiness Zones: 4–9

Mature Size: 40–60' tall x 40' wide

Habit: Upright oval

Growth Rate: Medium–fast

Bark: Exfoliating papery sheets of white, black, cinnamon, and cream shades

Leaf Color: Lustrous, medium to dark green

Fall Color: Yellow

Flowers: Catkins

Fruit: Small nutlet in spring

Disease & Insect Problems: None serious & highly resistant to bronze birch borer

Culture: Performs best in moist soils with pH of Ð 6.5 or chlorosis may occur; full to partial sun; will tolerate dry soils

Recommended Cultivars:
'BNMTF' (Dura-Heat®): smaller glossy leaves; heat-tolerant with yellow fall color
'Cully' (Heritage®): larger leaved, more exfoliation, and outstanding bark color
'Little King' (Fox Valley®): 10' tall x 12' wide; dense, compact, oval growth habit
'Shiloh Splash': smaller variegated leaves with irregular ivory–white leaf margins and green center
'Summer Cascade': pendulous, smaller cultivar reaching 10–20' tall
'Whit XXV' (City Slicker®): darker green leaf; superior drought and cold tolerance

Author Notes: This large, fine-textured, shade tree is also considered an ornamental because of its peeling bark. Some chlorosis may occur in high pH soils. Available as a multi-trunked form of three to five trunks, this fine specimen tree is perfect for areas along streams or ponds. The River Birch is a four-season plant.

Scientific Name: *Carpinus betulus*

Common Names: European Hornbeam
Common Hornbeam

Hardiness Zones: 4–7

Mature Size: 40' tall x 30' wide

Habit: Pyramidal to oval–rounded

Growth Rate: Medium

Bark: Ornamental, smooth, and slate gray; fluted; muscle-like

Leaf Color: Dark green

Fall Color: Yellow to yellow–green, and late

Flowers: Pendulous catkins in April

Fruit: Light brown nutlet in October

Disease & Insect Problems: None serious

Culture: Tolerant of many soil conditions, but must be well-drained; full sun

Recommended Cultivars:
   'Columnaris': retains its central leader and quite dense in habit
   'Fastigiata': upright growth; effective for screens and hedging
   'Frans Fontaine': unique central leader with inward-curving branches; maintains
     fastigiate form with maturity
   'Pendula': weeping, pendulous branching

Author Notes: This fine, medium-sized specimen tree is noted for its dense foliage
providing great symmetry and architectural value. It is also excellent for effective
year-round screens or hedges as it withstands pruning.

Scientific Name: *Carpinus caroliniana*

Common Names: American Hornbeam
Musclewood
Blue Beech
Ironwood

Hardiness Zones: 3–9

Mature Size: 25' tall & wide

Habit: Rounded multi-stemmed to single-stemmed with a wide spreading, flat-topped crown

Growth Rate: Slow

Bark: Muscle-like with smooth, blue–gray, fluted look; wood is hard and heavy

Leaf Color: Dark green

Fall Color: Yellow–orange–red, but variable

Flowers: Male and female on the same tree in April; female flowers are 4" long and attached to a three-winged bract and considered ornamental

Fruit: Small ribbed 1" nutlet that changes from green to brown in September and October

Disease & Insect Problems: Cankers and leaf diseases occur occasionally; some susceptiblity to native borer

Culture: Difficult to transplant; full sun, but prefers shade, and best in deep, moist, fertile, slightly acid, well-drained soils

Recommended Cultivar:
'CCSQU' (Palisade™): narrow oval outline; red fall color

Author Notes: This small understory tree is tolerant of a wide range of soil conditions. Typically found along streams and rivers, it is good in naturalized areas as it will tolerate periodic flooding. It is also tolerant of pruning and can be used as a hedge or screen. This tree is not drought-tolerant.

Scientific Name: *Cercidiphyllum japonicum*

Common Name: Katsuratree

Hardiness Zones: 4–8

Mature Size: 40–50' tall & wide

Habit: Pyramidal in youth becoming rounded with age

Growth Rate: Medium–fast

Bark: Shaggy and handsome brown on older trunks

Leaf Color: Emerge purple–red, then change to blue–green; heart-shaped like *Cercis*

Fall Color: Varying from yellow to apricot to occasionally orange–red; leaves release a warm and spicy fragrance, reminiscent of cotton candy

Flowers: Not showy

Fruit: Small narrow pod

Disease & Insect Problems: None serious but bark splitting and sun scald may occur

Culture: Grows best in moist, well-drained soil, pH adaptable; full sun but best in light shade; shallow root system, so supplemental watering required during hot, dry periods

Recommended Cultivars:
'Amazing Grace', 'Pendula': weeping habit reaching 20' tall and 20' wide
'Heronswood Globe': dwarf globe-shaped small tree, 15' tall, with a round crown
Morioka Weeping': beautiful weeping habit with a more upright form; stunning
'Red Fox', 'Rotfuchs': 25' tall with pronounced red–purple spring foliage and yellow–apricot fall color

Author Notes: This ornamental tree is grown for its delicate leaves and bright autumn color. Where conditions are suitable, it is fast growing, but it is very sensitive to drought and needs deep, permanently moist soil. Under drought conditions, the species will abscise its leaves, however refoliation may occur once water is made available. It should be somewhat protected and supplemented with irrigation if not protected. The scent produced by the leaves in the autumn resembles burnt brown sugar or cotton candy. It has a spreading habit and makes a good shade tree.

Scientific Name: *Cercis canadensis*

Common Name: Eastern Redbud

Hardiness Zones: 4–9

Mature Size: 15–25' tall & wide

Habit: Upright–vase shaped

Growth Rate: Fast in youth, then slowing to medium

Bark: Somewhat ornamental with orange inner bark and brown–black outer bark

Leaf Color: Emerging red–purple and changing to dark green; heart-shaped

Fall Color: Yellow–green to yellow

Flowers: Bright lavender in April before leaves emerge

Fruit: Brown pod 2–3" long in October

Disease & Insect Problems: Canker is most destructive disease; some Verticillium wilt

Culture: Prefers moist, well-drained soil; does not tolerate wet feet; adaptable to pH; full sun to partial shade

Recommended Cultivars:
'Covey' (Lavender Twist™): small weeping form with umbrella-like crown
'Floating Clouds': white variegated leaf and pink flowers
'Forest Pansy': leaves emerge red–purple; intense rose–purple flowers
'Greswan' (Burgundy Hearts®): retains its deep wine color throughout end of season
'Hearts of Gold': leaves emerge yellow tinted with red–purple maturing to yellow
'JN2' (The Rising Sun™): lemon yellow to apricot foliage into the fall
'Royal White': white flowers with more cold hardiness

Author Notes: This popular, small ornamental tree has showy spring flowers. Eastern Redbud is a strikingly conspicuous tree in the spring because it flowers before other tree leaves form. It is best for naturalized, woodland (understory) settings. Unfortunately, this is not a long-lived tree as the life span is typically 15–20 years.

Scientific Name: *Chionanthus virginicus*

Common Name: White Fringetree

Hardiness Zones: 4–9

Mature Size: 10–20' tall & wide

Habit: Spreading with variable shapes

Growth Rate: Slow

Bark: Smooth gray in youth, becoming slightly furrowed

Leaf Color: Medium green; extremely late to leaf out (mid-May)

Fall Color: Yellow to brown

Flowers: White, slight fragrance after foliage expands; fleecy, drooping 6–8" panicles in late May to early June; outstanding

Fruit: Dark blue drupe ripening in September and prized by animals; dioecious, so fruit only on females; plant one male to two female

Disease & Insect Problems: None serious

Culture: Prefers deep, moist, acidic soil but is adaptable; full sun to partial shade

Recommended Cultivars: None

Author Notes: This is one of the best small, native-American, flowering plants. When in bloom, the sights and smells are incredible. Commonly multi-trunked, the White Fringetree can be pruned to a single-stem form and makes a great specimen tree/shrub. It is great for naturalized areas as a group or border planting, preferring afternoon shade.

Scientific Name: *Cladrastis kentukea (lutea)*

Common Name: American Yellowwood

Hardiness Zones: 4–8

Mature Size: 30–50' tall & wide

Habit: Rounded vase, with low branching

Growth Rate: Medium

Bark: Thin, gray, and resembling beech; beautiful

Leaf Color: Opening bright yellow–green and gradually turning to bright green

Fall Color: Yellow to golden yellow

Flowers: White (long panicles), fragrant, and ornamental in June

Fruit: Tan–brown pod in October

Disease & Insect Problems: None serious

Culture: Best in full sun and likes well-drained soil; adaptable to pH

Recommended Cultivar:
'Rosea': handsome pink-flowered form

Author Notes: This choice medium ornamental shade tree is excellent as a specimen or in groupings. Gray beech-like bark on its vase-shaped form coupled with a nice yellow fall color makes this an attractive choice. Flowers attract bees; prune only in the summer as it is a profuse bleeder. Occasional problematic bad crotches can split in windstorms.

Scientific Name: *Cornus alternifolia*

Common Names: Pagoda Dogwood
Alternate-leaf Dogwood

Hardiness Zones: 3–7

Mature Size: 15–20' tall & wide

Habit: Spreading with horizontal low branching; distinguished look year-round

Growth Rate: Slow initially, then medium with age

Bark: Younger stems are shiny brown to purple; gray and slightly ridged when older

Leaf Color: Dark green

Fall Color: Red to deep red but variable; rarely outstanding

Flowers: Fragrant white–yellow produced in clusters during late spring; attractive

Fruit: Handsome blue–black drupe on pink–red stalk in midsummer; berries are a valuable food for birds and other wildlife

Disease & Insect Problems: Susceptible to a number of diseases, including twig blights and cankers; appears to be resistant to dogwood anthracnose, which in recent years has killed many *Cornus florida* (Flowering Dogwoods)

Culture: Full sun or part shade but usually looks and performs better in light shade; requires slightly-acid, moist, well-drained soil; protect from harsh winter winds

Recommended Cultivars:
'Argentea': leaves with a creamy white variegation and a compact form
'W. Stackman' (Golden Shadows®): striking foliage exhibiting a defined green center surrounded by a yellow–gold band; consistent coloring for a variegated plant

Author Notes: This small understory tree is native to much of the eastern United States. It gets its common name from its pagoda-like, horizontal, branching pattern. The interesting branching structure gives the plant winter appeal. It seems to do best in colder climates; the key to success is keeping the root zone cool, moist, and acidic. During dry spells it is advised to water young plants. Pagoda Dogwood is an alternative to *C. florida*.

Scientific Name: *Cornus florida*

Common Name: Flowering Dogwood

Hardiness Zones: 5–9

Mature Size: 15' tall x 20' wide

Habit: Upright oval, with low-branching and horizontal spread

Growth Rate: Slow

Bark: Gray to dark brown, with small rectangular blocks

Leaf Color: Medium–dark green

Fall Color: Red to purple

Flowers: Inconspicuous green–yellow; white bracts are showy in May

Fruit: Glossy red drupe ripening in October; birds love to devour

Disease & Insect Problems: Many including borer, anthracnose, and powdery mildew

Culture: Prefers acid, well-drained site to maintain cool, moist soil; best in partial shade

Recommended Cultivars:
'Cherokee Chief': deep red flowers; foliage emerges red, then becomes green
'Cloud Nine': large white flowers; red fall color
'Grovflor' (Spring Grove®): extra large white flowers; red–purple fall color with good cold hardiness
'Sunset', 'Cherokee Sunset' (Cherokee Sunset™): red flowers; foliage emerges green with dark pink margin, changing to a creamy margin; pink–purple fall color
Subspecies *urbiniana* 'Magic Dogwood': very unique form; funky, spiral, white bracts are fused at tips forming a Chinese lantern shape; blue–green leaves

Author Notes: This aristocratic small tree has four-season appeal. It tends to be short-lived in urban areas due to adaptation issues like alkaline and dry soils. This is a native understory tree that is best used as a specimen or in groupings. The pink and red "flower" selections are usually not cold hardy.

Scientific Name: *Cornus kousa*

Common Names: Kousa Dogwood
Chinese Dogwood

Hardiness Zones: 5–8

Mature Size: 20–25′ tall & wide

Habit: Vase shape in youth, becoming rounded with age

Growth Rate: Slow

Bark: Mottled cream–gray, with some exfoliation

Leaf Color: Dark blue–green

Fall Color: Burgundy in late autumn

Flowers: Inconspicuous; bracts are creamy white in June and appear after leafing out

Fruit: Pink–red, raspberry-like drupe in September to October

Disease & Insect Problems: None serious

Culture: Adaptable to varying soil pH; prefers well-drained soil doing best in full sun, but will do better with afternoon shade

Recommended Cultivars:
'Lustgarten Weeping': weeping form mainly on upper branches; distinctive
'Samzam' (Samaritan®): hardy and variegated with abundant star-shaped flowers
'Satomi': pink–red bracts; slow grower
'Wolf Eyes': white margined leaves with impressive pink–red fall color
Cornus x 'Rutgan' (Constellation®): long white bracts
Cornus x 'Rutgan' (Stellar Pink®): rounded soft-pink bracts
Cornus x 'Rutgan' (Variegated Stellar Pink™): new with green leaves and white margins; variegated

Author Notes: A handsome, small, ornamental, four-season tree with layered branching, Kousa is a more drought-resistant and dependable alternative than *C. florida* (Flowering Dogwood). Use as a specimen or seasonal accent tree. Many cultivars are available in the trade. There are new hybrids of *C. kousa* x *C. florida* developed at Rutgers University by Dr. Elwin Orton that exhibit rounded bracts, resistance to dogwood anthracnose, more vigor and erect habit, and have no fruit as the plants are sterile.

Scientific Name: *Cornus mas*

Common Name: Corneliancherry Dogwood

Hardiness Zones: 4–8

Mature Size: 20' tall & wide

Habit: Oval–rounded

Growth Rate: Medium

Bark: Exfoliating, flaky, with gray–brown colors

Leaf Color: Dark green and glossy

Fall Color: Variable, can be purple–red, but leaves may drop green, too, in late fall

Flowers: Yellow in March before leaves; signal that spring has arrived

Fruit: Bright cherry–red oblong drupe in July; have seen the fruit used for jelly, jam, and to make wine

Disease & Insect Problems: None serious

Culture: Adaptable to varying soil types and pH; best in well-drained, rich soil; full sun to partial shade

Recommended Cultivars:
'Aureo-Elegantissima', 'Elegantissima': variegated leaves of yellow, pink, and green
'Flava': yellow fruits that are larger and sweeter
'Golden Glory': more upright form and profuse flowering; dark green leaves
'Pyramidalis': upright version with spread of 10'
'Redstone': abundant large red fruit
'Variegata': showy bark; variegated white–green foliage

Author Notes: This is an excellent small ornamental tree or large ornamental shrub. A very durable and underutilized dogwood, it is typically multi-trunked with branching close to the ground. It is effective as a screen, hedge, or border, and is superb as an early-spring-flowering specimen. The Corneliancherry Dogwood is a harbinger of spring.

Scientific Name: *Fagus sylvatica*

Common Name: European Beech

Hardiness Zones: 4–7

Mature Size: 50–60' tall x 35–45' wide

Habit: Upright oval

Growth Rate: Slow

Bark: Smooth, gray, and darker than American Beech; ornamental in winter

Leaf Color: Shimmering green, changing to dark green; emerges late

Fall Color: Golden bronze

Flowers: April to May, with leaves

Fruit: Triangular nuts in four-lobed spiny husks; October

Disease & Insect Problems: Few

Culture: Ideally suited in full sun to part-shade; prefers deep well-drained soil

Recommended Cultivars:
  'Asplenifolia': fine-textured form; cut leaves that turn golden brown fall color
  'Dawyck Purple': purple-foliaged upright, columnar form
  'Pendula': weeping form, but no two are alike
  'Purpurea Tricolor', 'Tricolor': outstanding purple foliage with irregular cream and
    rose borders; loses color as season goes on

Author Notes: It would be difficult to find a finer specimen tree. This large, graceful, four-season shade tree is more tolerant of compacted soils than *F. grandifolia* (American Beech) although there may be some surface roots with age. It naturally branches close to the ground. There are many cultivars to pick from for growth habit and varied foliage.

Scientific Name: *Franklinia alatamaha*

Common Names: Franklinia
Franklin Tree

Hardiness Zones: 5–8

Mature Size: 10–20' tall x 10' wide

Habit: Upright

Growth Rate: Medium

Bark: Attractive, smooth gray, with irregular vertical fissures

Leaf Color: Lustrous bright green to dark green

Fall Color: Orange–red and usually hold leaves late; vivid

Flowers: Striking fragrant 3" white petals and yellow–orange stamens in late summer

Fruit: Brown, five-valved, woody capsule

Disease & Insect Problems: Wilt caused by *Phytophthora* root rot

Culture: Requires humus-rich, moist, acid, well-drained soil; full sun to part shade with best flowering and fall color occurring in full sun; water it during dry spells, especially when young

Recommended Cultivars: None

Author Notes: This small aristocratic specimen tree is valued for its showy white flowers and reasonably good fall color. Cultivated specimens of Franklinia are commonly bushy plants, often with multiple trunks like a shrub, but they can usually be trained into tree form. This historical tree is indeed fickle. Good drainage is essential and, in cold climates, the plant may die back to the ground. Many gardeners wax poetically about this plant, but very few seem to have one in their own garden.

Scientific Name: *Ginkgo biloba*

Common Names: Ginkgo
Maidenhair Tree

Hardiness Zones: 4–9

Mature Size: 60–80' tall x 40–60' wide

Habit: Upright columnar

Growth Rate: Slow–medium

Bark: Gray–brown with dark furrows; distinctive and handsome

Leaf Color: Bright green and fan-shaped

Fall Color: Yellow in November; one of the finest

Flowers: Green; March to April; catkins

Fruit: Naked seed; fleshy covering and rank odor; female trees

Disease & Insect Problems: None

Culture: Prefers deep, sandy soil but adaptable to stressful situations and pH levels

Recommended Cultivars:
'Autumn Gold': non-fruiting male; symmetrical; golden fall color
'Princeton Sentry': columnar, upright form
'Saratoga': non-fruiting male; distinct central leader
'The President' (Presidential Gold®): bright yellow fall color; full, dense habit

Author Notes: This excellent large shade and ornamental tree is very urban tolerant and bold textured. Be patient as it will evolve into a spectacular specimen or focal point tree. A gymnosperm, the Gingko is one of the oldest trees growing on earth; it is highly recommended to purchase and plant the non-fruiting male species only.

Scientific Name: *Gleditsia triacanthos* var. *inermis*

Common Name: Thornless Honeylocust

Hardiness Zones: 4–9

Mature Size: 60' tall x 40' wide

Habit: Upright oval

Growth Rate: Fast

Bark: Gray–brown with vertical fissures

Leaf Color: Bright green

Fall Color: Yellow; drop early in autumn

Flowers: Green–yellow in May to June; slightly fragrant and nectar-laden

Fruit: Long pods; red–brown–black in fall

Disease & Insect Problems: Numerous problems including canker, rust, borer, webworm

Culture: Tolerant of a wide range of conditions including drought and high pH; full sun; very urban tolerant

Recommended Cultivars:
'Harve' (Northern Acclaim®): broad pyramidal; seedless
'Impcole' (Imperial®): spreading habit, with bright green leaves
'Shademaster' (Shademaster®): open, rounded canopy; sturdy and strong grower
'Skycole' (Skyline®): pyramidal, with bright yellow fall color; adaptable
'Suncole' (Sunburst®): pyramidal; emerging foliage brilliant yellow, fading to a light green; urban tolerant

Author Notes: This is one of the most adaptable large trees providing filtered summer shade and minimal leaf litter. Surface roots can be a problem; always prune in the fall. This honeylocust provides a beautiful winter outline, but is somewhat overused and has a few problems.

Scientific Name: *Gymnocladus dioicus*

Common Name: Kentucky Coffeetree

Hardiness Zones: 4–8

Mature Size: 60–75' tall x 40–50' wide

Habit: Irregular growth in youth, becoming upright rounded

Growth Rate: Slow–medium

Bark: Rough; gray–brown to dark brown scaly plates

Leaf Color: Emerging purple-tinged, then becoming dark green; late to leaf out; mid–May

Fall Color: Ineffective; some yellow

Flowers: White–green in late May to early June

Fruit: Leathery pods; red–brown in October; tend to hang on through winter

Disease & Insect Problems: None serious

Culture: Best in deep, rich, moist limestone soils but very adaptable; full sun

Recommended Cultivars:
    'Espresso-JFS' (Espresso™): male (fruitless)
    'Stately Manor': male (fruitless)

Author Notes: This choice, large tree provides semi-filtered shade and a beautiful, bold, winter canopy. Older trees are majestic and handsome. It can get somewhat dirty with the pods and leaflets; prune only in winter/early spring. This tree is dioecious so the males do not fruit. It is tolerant to heat, drought, and cold.

Scientific Name: *Halesia carolina (tetraptera)*

Common Name: Carolina Silverbell

Hardiness Zones: 5–8

Mature Size: 30' tall x 20' wide

Habit: Conical, typically low-branched, and single-trunked

Growth Rate: Medium

Bark: Trunk is brown to gray with furrows; young branches are smooth gray–brown with prominent darker striations

Leaf Color: Dark green

Fall Color: Yellow–green, dropping early

Flowers: White, pendulous, bell-shaped clusters on year-old wood in late April to early May

Fruit: Four-winged, oblong, dry drupe; lime green changing to brown; abscises in fall but still ornamentally effective

Disease & Insect Problems: None serious

Culture: Full sun to part shade; prefers rich, acid, well-drained, moist soils in a partial shade environment; tolerant of fairly heavy shade

Recommended Cultivars:
'Arnold Pink': pink flowers
'Lady Catherine': weeping form
'Rosea': light pink flowers

Author Notes: This small understory woodland tree has a native habitat on wooded slopes and along stream banks in the central and southern United States. It exhibits a prolific mid-spring blossom of white, bell-shaped flowers that hang from the branches. Once difficult to find, the Carolina Silverbell is now, fortunately, being propagated by a number of nurseries, thereby increasing its availability. As more people plant this tree, eventually it will get the appreciation it deserves.

Scientific Name: *Heptacodium miconioides*

Common Name: Seven-son Flower

Hardiness Zones: 5–8

Mature Size: 15–20' tall x 10' wide

Habit: Upright, but in a loose, irregular manner

Growth Rate: Medium

Bark: Showy, shredding, gray–light brown in thin strips that peel back

Leaf Color: Glossy, dark green

Fall Color: Muted yellow to purple–bronze; usually holds leaves late

Flowers: Fragrant, creamy white in August to September on 6" long terminal panicles

Fruit: Purple–red round capsule enclosed by bright purple–red calyces (sepals)

Disease & Insect Problems: None serious

Culture: Full sun to light shade with fertile, well-drained soil; adaptable but may need supplemental watering during dry periods

Recommended Cultivars: None

Author Notes: Introduced to this country by the Arnold Arboretum and U.S. National Arboretum from China, the Seven-son Flower is a beautiful multi-stemmed shrub or small tree. Its tan bark exfoliates to reveal an attractive brown inner bark reminding me of an old honeysuckle plant. In late summer the white flowers open with a fragrance similar to jasmine. In fall, the ornamental calyx turns bright purple–red and lasts until the first hard frost. This is a great plant choice for late summer, fall, and winter interest and also attracts butterflies and many bees during flowering.

Scientific Name: *Koelreuteria paniculata*

Common Names: Panicled Goldenraintree
Varnish Tree

Hardiness Zones: 5–9

Mature Size: 30' tall & wide

Habit: Upright rounded

Growth Rate: Medium–fast

Bark: Light gray–brown with furrows as tree ages

Leaf Color: Emerging purple-toned, then turning bright green

Fall Color: Inconsistent but some yellow to yellow orange

Flowers: Showy yellow 12–15" panicles in early July

Fruit: Three-sided brown pods about 2" long containing one to three round black seeds; may persist through winter

Disease & Insect Problems: None serious

Culture: Very adaptable to soil conditions; withstands drought; full sun

Recommended Cultivars:
'Coral Sun': produces orange–red new growth that eventually fades to green
'Rose Lantern': exhibits pink seedpods during summer
'September': abundant producer of yellow flowers

Author Notes: This medium ornamental or shade tree is unrivaled for yellow flowers in summer months and its urban tolerance. It is an excellent street tree. (There are two in the author's front yard.) It was selected as the 2011 SMA (Society of Municipal Arborists) tree of the year. I believe this to be a very deserving award as this has been the Rodney Dangerfield of trees.

Scientific Name: *Liriodendron tulipifera*

Common Names: Tuliptree
Tulip Poplar
Yellow Poplar

Hardiness Zones: 4–9

Mature Size: 70–90' tall x 35–50' wide

Habit: Pyramidal to oval–rounded

Growth Rate: Fast

Bark: In youth, smooth and gray; develops deep furrows with age and easily recognized

Leaf Color: Green and somewhat glossy; unique four-lobed shape

Fall Color: Yellow to golden yellow in October to early November

Flowers: Six beautiful green–yellow petals in mid-May to mid-June

Fruit: Cone-like samaras 2–3Ð long that turn brown in October and persist through winter

Disease & Insect Problems: Several minor insect and disease problems, notably aphids causing some cosmetic issues

Culture: Prefers deep, moist, well-drained loamy soil; full sun; pH adaptable; prune in winter

Recommended Cultivars:
'Ardis': smaller version with everything about one-third the size; 25' mature height
'Aureomarginata': visually striking, margined leaves of yellow and green
'Glen Gold': new leaves are bright yellow; 50' tall
'Little Volunteer': upright, medium size; 35" tall

Author Notes: This large, fast-growing shade tree produces showy, tulip-like flowers; flowering usually begins at 15 years of age. It is one of the largest shade trees with a strong central leader. Exceptional when planted in large groupings or groves, the Tuliptree's twig and small-branch litter are messy, especially in small yards. Smaller cultivars are now available to incorporate into a landscape where the species is just too large.

Scientific Name: *Magnolia acuminata*

Common Names: Cucumbertree Magnolia
Cucumber Magnolia

Hardiness Zones: 4–8

Mature Size: 50–70' tall & wide

Habit: Pyramidal in youth, to rounded at maturity

Growth Rate: Medium–fast

Bark: Smooth gray–brown in youth; ridged and furrowed with age

Leaf Color: Dark green and large

Fall Color: Not exciting, but a few will exhibit a soft ash-brown

Flowers: Green–yellow petals in May to early June; slightly fragrant

Fruit: Pink–red in October resembling 2–3Ð small cucumber

Disease & Insect Problems: None serious

Culture: Prefers deep, loamy, well-drained soils; performs well in the calcareous soils of the Midwest; partial shade to full sun; not tolerable of extreme drought or wetness

Recommended Cultivars:
'Butterflies': deep yellow flowers before the foliage, fading to creamy white; hybrid magnolia (*acuminata* x *denudata*); 20' mature height
'Daybreak': slightly fragrant pink flowers open with the foliage; 35' tall x 20' wide
'Elizabeth': pale yellow flowers before the foliage; hybrid magnolia (*acuminata* x *denudata*); 40' mature height

Author Notes: This is an excellent large shade tree that provides great character for larger properties. It is the hardiest of the native *Magnolia* species. Nursery-grown cultivars have showy yellow flowers and are becoming easier to find. These make fine specimen trees for the landscape.

Scientific Name: *Magnolia stellata*

Common Name: Star Magnolia

Hardiness Zones: 4–8

Mature Size: 15–20' tall & wide

Habit: Oval–rounded

Growth Rate: Slow

Bark: Gray, smooth, and handsome on mature plants

Leaf Color: Dark green

Fall Color: Green–yellow; not exciting

Flowers: White, slight fragrance in April before leaves

Fruit: Not distinguishable

Disease & Insect Problems: None serious

Culture: As with most magnolias, some form of protection is best; full sun to partial shade; tolerant of soil types and pH

Recommended Cultivars:
'Centennial': wide flowers; vigorous and cold hardy
'Royal Star': earliest bloomer with pink buds opening to fragrant white flowers

Author Notes: This small, upright, multi-trunked tree or shrub has showy white flowers that are frequently browned by early spring frosts. The Star Magnolia, used mainly as a specimen or accent tree, is another harbinger of spring.

Scientific Name: *Magnolia virginiana*

Common Names: Sweetbay Magnolia
Laurel Magnolia

Hardiness Zones: 5–9

Mature Size: 10–20' tall x 15' wide

Habit: Upright oval

Growth Rate: Slow–medium

Bark: Light gray and smooth

Leaf Color: Dark green and elliptical with silver underside

Fall Color: Yellow to yellow–brown

Flowers: Creamy white and wonderful lemon scent; 2–3" in May to June, often continuing until September

Fruit: Dark red seeds, 2" long, ripening in September

Disease & Insect Problems: None serious

Culture: Prefers acidic soils; full sun to full shade; tolerant of wet soils

Recommended Cultivars:
'Green Shadow': upright form; evergreen and cold hardy
'Jim Wilson' (Moonglow®): upright and taller; dark green foliage; semi-evergreen

Author Notes: This upright, small, multi-trunked tree with graceful, lateral branching is prone to chlorosis in alkaline soil. A North American native, it offers lovely, lemon-scented flowers throughout summer. Place this magnolia near a window to enjoy the fragrance.

Scientific Name: *Malus species*

Common Name: Flowering Crabapple

Hardiness Zones: 4–8

Mature Size: 15–25' tall & wide

Habit: Various

Growth Rate: Medium

Bark: Smooth when young; lightly furrowed and often knotty with age

Leaf Color: Green to dark green

Fall Color: Usually insignificant

Flowers: White, pink, or red; typically single-flowered before foliage in April to May

Fruit: Red, orange, yellow, or green in showy clusters September to October; some persist into December

Disease & Insect Problems: Fireblight, cedar apple rust, and apple scab to name a few problems mainly on older cultivars that have been removed from sale; lead to premature defoliation and fruit drop

Culture: Adaptable to varying soils, but good drainage is a must; pH adaptable; drought and heavy pruning tolerant

Recommended Cultivars: Modern cultivars below have been selected because they flower annually, have persistent fruit, and exhibit tolerance or resistance to most of the pests and diseases that plague crabapples. Some favorites:

'Adirondack': vase; crimson buds; white flowers; orange–red fruits.
'Bob White': rounded; pink buds; white flowers; yellow fruits.
'Candymint': low spreading; deep pink buds; rose pink flowers; red fruits.
'Cinzam' (Cinderella®): upright compact; red buds; white flowers; golden yellow fruits.
'Excazam' (Excalibur™): rounded; light pink buds; white flowers; light golden yellow fruits.
'Guinzam' (Guinevere®): rounded, wide spreading; red buds; white flowers; bright red fruits.
'Hozam' (Holiday Gold™): open rounded; pink buds; white flowers; yellow fruits with red blush.
'Jewelcole' (Red Jewel®): upright spreading; white buds; white flowers; cherry red fruits.
'Lanzam' (Lancelot®): upright compact; red buds; white flowers; golden yellow fruits.
'Lollipop': dwarf rounded; red buds; white flowers; golden amber fruits.
'Louisa': weeping; red buds; true pink flowers; yellow fruits.
'Orange Crush': rounded; deep burgundy buds; red flowers; orange–red fruits.
'Prairifire': upright spreading; crimson buds; dark red flowers; purple–red fruits.
'Pumpkin Pie': upright oval; pink buds; white flowers; striking yellow fruits.
Sargentii (Sargent's Apple): dwarf spreading shrub; pale pink buds; white flowers; red fruits.
'Select A' (Firebird®): rounded spreading; red–pink buds; white flowers; bright orange–red fruits.
'Tina': dwarf, tightly compacted and shrubby; red–pink buds; white flowers; dark red fruits

Author Notes: This small-to-medium, spring-flowering, ornamental tree is mainly used for specimens. It is known for its spectacular spring flowering, varied growth habits and sizes, autumn-to-winter fruits, and urban tolerance. Beware of basal suckers, water sprouts, crossing branches that require pruning to keep neat look and vigor, and winter fruit litter in non-lawn areas. In the Midwest, there is no finer small ornamental tree.

Scientific Name: *Nyssa sylvatica*

Common Names: Black Tupelo
Black Gum
Sour Gum

Hardiness Zones: 4–9

Mature Size: 30–50' tall x 20–30' wide

Habit: Pyramidal

Growth Rate: Slow–medium

Bark: Dark gray–brown with blocky (rectangular) appearance

Leaf Color: Dark green, shiny, and elliptical

Fall Color: Outstanding fluorescent yellow, orange, scarlet, and purple

Flowers: Not effective or ornamentally significant

Fruit: Oblong blue–black drupe in late September to early October; favorite of birds
and squirrels

Disease & Insect Problems: Some leaf spot causing cosmetic damage

Culture: Best in deep, moist, well-drained, acid soils; full sun to partial shade;
fall prune

Recommended Cultivars:
'Autumn Cascades': semi-weeping, female form; blue–black fruit; yellow–orange–
red fall color
'Hayman Red' (Red Rage®): dark green, lustrous foliage; excellent red fall color
'Tupelo Tower': exhibits a tight, upright, narrow habit; a Klyn Nurseries
introduction
'Wildfire': new foliage emerges deep red; fall color array of yellow–orange–
scarlet red–purple
'Zydeco Twist': contorted, spiraling stems make interesting habit; vivid red fall color

Author Notes: An excellent large shade tree, the Black Tupelo is mainly used as a
specimen. This is one of the best and most consistent native trees for fall color
but is not to be planted in alkaline soils. Underutilized, it has lustrous, dark
green, summer foliage with consistently striking autumn color. There can be
some variability in its growth habit as most tupelos are upright but a few cascade.

Scientific Name: *Ostrya virginiana*

Common Names: American Hophornbeam
Ironwood

Hardiness Zones: 4–9

Mature Size: 25–40' tall x 25' wide

Habit: Rounded with upright and spreading branching

Growth Rate: Slow

Bark: Gray–brown with vertical strips which exfoliate at the ends

Leaf Color: Dark green and sharply serrated

Fall Color: Yellow, but not particularly effective

Flowers: Catkins in April to May

Fruit: Flattened nutlet inside an enclosed pod in clusters; fruit clusters look like fruit of hops, thus the common name of Hophornbeam; fruits change from green to tan

Disease & Insect Problems: None serious

Culture: Full sun to part shade and best in slightly acid soil that is cool, moist, and well-drained; slow to establish following transplanting, but once established it can tolerate dry, gravelly soil in part shade

Recommended Cultivars: None

Author Notes: This attractive, small-to-medium sized, understory tree is a slow grower. It does well on dry sites and, once established, grows very well. The American Hophornbeam is not tolerant of salt, so avoid roadside plantings, but use for lawns, parks, golf courses, and, especially, in naturalized areas. This tree can be difficult to find in the nursery trade but it is worth the search.

Scientific Name: *Oxydendrum arboreum*

Common Names: Sourwood
Lily of the Valley Tree
Sorrel Tree

Hardiness Zones: 5–9

Mature Size: 25' tall x 20' wide; 50–75' tall in the wild

Habit: Pyramidal

Growth Rate: Slow

Bark: Thick, deep-furrowed, gray–brown with scaly ridges that are often broken into rectangles; similar to the blocky appearance of persimmon

Leaf Color: Lustrous green to dark green

Fall Color: Yellow–orange–red–purple

Flowers: White, ¼" long, urn-shaped, and fragrant on drooping panicles; reminiscent of lily-of-the-valley flowers; midsummer

Fruit: Five-valved, brown capsule on panicles

Disease & Insect Problems: None serious

Culture: Full sun to part shade; best flowering and fall color occurs in sun; prefers a slightly acid, moist, well-drained, humus soil

Recommended Cultivar: None

Author Notes: This attractive tree is occasionally used as an ornamental because of its brilliant fall color and midsummer flowers. In the right location and under the correct conditions, this can be a spectacular specimen plant. It is not tolerant to urban environments or alkaline soils and requires watering during hot, dry summers. Sourwood is important as a source of honey in some areas and is marketed locally.

Scientific Name: *Parrotia persica*

Common Names: Persian Parrotia
Persian Ironwood

Hardiness Zones: 4–8

Mature Size: 30' tall x 20' wide

Habit: Oval rounded

Growth Rate: Medium

Bark: Some exfoliation on older trunks exposing a mosaic of gray, brown, white, and green

Leaf Color: Unfolding red–purple, then changing to a shiny dark green

Fall Color: Beautiful yellow to orange to scarlet colors when exposed to full sun

Flowers: Red stamens in April but insignificant

Fruit: Capsule; ornamentally ineffective

Disease & Insect Problems: None serious

Culture: Prefers well-drained, loamy soils; full sun to partial shade; tolerant of some high pH; extremely tolerant; prune in spring

Recommended Cultivars:
'Biltmore': low branching; rounded habit; fabulous bark
'Jennifer Teates': upright form, with tight ascending branching; heat-tolerant
'Ruby Vase': columnar form with early leaves ruby red with orange–purple fall colors
'Vanessa': upright columnar; vivid yellow fall color

Author Notes: One of the best specimen trees, the Persian Parrotia is known for its foliage, bark, and pest resistance. This outstanding small ornamental tree has few rivals. It is typically low branched. This fine, four-season plant should be used more extensively in landscapes, parks, and golf courses. Author has an 11-year-old tight upright form (likely 'Vanessa') and marvels at the beauty of the tree in all 12 months of the year. It has been selected as the 2014 SMA (Society of Municipal Arborists) urban tree of the year.

Scientific Name: *Quercus acutissima*

Common Name: Sawtooth Oak

Hardiness Zones: 5–8

Mature Size: 40–50' tall & wide

Habit: Pyramidal in youth, becoming rounded with age

Growth Rate: Medium–fast

Bark: Brown with deep furrows; cork-like appearance

Leaf Color: Dark, glossy green, with serrated bristle-like teeth

Fall Color: Clear yellow to golden yellow in November

Flowers: 3–4" catkins in early April

Fruit: Acorn

Disease & Insect Problems: None serious

Culture: Prefers acid, well-drained soil, but is adaptable; may develop chlorosis in high pH soil; performs well in heat; full sun

Recommended Cultivars: None

Author Notes: This is a handsome, clean-foliaged, large shade tree. The new leaves emerge bright yellow in the spring and exude a radiant glow to the entire tree. Another underutilized tree in the landscape, this oak can be a prolific bearer of acorns. The flowers of oaks are noticeable but not ornamental. The Sawtooth transplants more easily than most oaks.

Scientific Name: *Quercus bicolor*

Common Name: Swamp White Oak

Hardiness Zones: 3–8

Mature Size: 50–60' tall & wide

Habit: Upright oval in youth, becoming rounded with age

Growth Rate: Medium

Bark: Brown; notable flared bark feature exhibiting bold winter texture

Leaf Color: Dark green, with white–green undersides

Fall Color: Moderate yellow to yellow–brown, with an occasional red–purple

Flowers: Yellow–brown catkins in late April; insignificant

Fruit: Acorn

Disease & Insect Problems: None serious

Culture: Full sun in moist-to-wet, deep acid soils; adaptable to dry soils

Recommended Cultivars: None

Author Notes: This large, rounded, shade tree is noted for its bicolor foliage in the wind, ornamental bark, and bold texture in the winter. It is also adaptable to wet or dry sites. The Swamp White Oak is becoming more readily available and is easier to transplant than most oaks.

Scientific Name: *Quercus imbricaria*

Common Names: Shingle Oak
Laurel Oak

Hardiness Zones: 4–7

Mature Size: 60' tall x 70' wide

Habit: Upright oval in youth, becoming rounded and spreading with age

Growth Rate: Medium

Bark: Gray–brown, with shallow furrows

Leaf Color: Glossy, dark green, with lobeless oblong leaves

Fall Color: Yellow–brown to russet brown; usually persist into winter

Flowers: Yellow–brown catkins in late April

Fruit: Acorn (small)

Disease & Insect Problems: None serious

Culture: Prefers moist, rich, deep, well-drained. acid soil; full sun; adaptable to poor soils, dry soils, and varying pH levels

Recommended Cultivars: None

Author Notes: This large, spreading, shade tree performs well in dry sites. It has leaves that shine like laurel. The Shingle Oak is also very cold hardy and urban tolerant. A good tree for street and park uses, this is another oak that is relatively easy to transplant.

Scientific Name: *Quercus muehlenbergii*

Common Names: Chinkapin Oak
Yellow Chestnut Oak

Hardiness Zones: 4–7

Mature Size: 40–50' tall x 55' wide; 70–80' tall in the wild

Habit: Rounded

Growth Rate: Slow–medium

Bark: Ash light gray with some flaking

Leaf Color: Glossy, dark green, with sharp pointed teeth

Fall Color: Variable from yellow to orange to brown

Flowers: Yellow catkins in May; attractive

Fruit: Acorn; dark brown–black in late fall

Disease & Insect Problems: None serious

Culture: Full sun in rich, well-drained, alkaline soils; drought tolerant

Recommended Cultivars: None

Author Notes: A worthy specimen for larger lawns, golf courses, estates, or parks, the Chinkapin is adaptable to many different soil types. This medium- to large-sized oak has sweet acorns that are at the top of the food preference list for many wildlife species. Although it is difficult to find in the nursery trade because of transplanting difficulty, it may be the most alkaline-soil-tolerant oak. As it matures, this tree becomes a magnificent specimen and a conversation piece.

Scientific Name: *Quercus palustris*

Common Name: Pin Oak

Hardiness Zones: 4–7

Mature Size: 60–70' tall x 25–40' wide; 100' tall in nature

Habit: Upright pyramidal

Growth Rate: Medium–fast

Bark: Gray–brown and smooth in youth, but developing narrow and shallow furrows

Leaf Color: Glossy, dark green

Fall Color: Bronze to crimson red

Flowers: Yellow–brown catkins in late April; insignificant

Fruit: Acorn (small)

Disease & Insect Problems: Galls sometimes a problem, but not too serious

Culture: Shallow, fibrous, root systems allow easy transplanting; tolerant of wet soils; best in moist, rich, acid, well-drained soils; intolerant of high pH; full sun

Recommended Cultivar:

'Pringreen' (Green Pillar®): columnar; leaves are extremely lustrous

Author Notes: Strongly pyramidal in youth, this is a very popular large shade tree that tolerates wet or dry sites. Characteristics include downswept lower branches and ascending upper branches. If planted in low pH (acid) soils, the tree can grow rapidly. Planting in high pH (alkaline) soils will promote iron chlorosis.

Scientific Name: *Quercus rubra*

Common Names: Red Oak
Eastern Red Oak
Northern Red Oak

Hardiness Zones: 4–7

Mature Size: 60–75′ tall & wide

Habit: Upright oval in youth, becoming rounded with age

Growth Rate: Medium–fast

Bark: Brown to black; ridged and furrowed

Leaf Color: Lustrous, dark green; spring growth is bronze–red

Fall Color: Russet red to bright red; sometimes disappointing

Flowers: Catkins in late April

Fruit: Acorn (large)

Disease & Insect Problems: None serious

Culture: Prefers acid, well-drained, loamy soils; full sun; may get some chlorosis in high pH soils

Recommended Cultivar:

'Aurea': exhibits yellow leaves maturing to green

Author Notes: A large shade tree that often excels in dry sites, the Red Oak has a decent brick-red fall color. Fruit litter may be a problem. Because of its negligible taproot, this is one of the easiest oaks to transplant and one of the most prominent trees in the United States. It is also one of the largest and most important timber trees.

Scientific Name: *Quercus shumardii*

Common Name: Shumard Oak

Hardiness Zones: 5–9

Mature Size: 50' tall & wide in landscape; 100' tall in nature

Habit: Pyramidal to rounded

Growth Rate: Medium

Bark: Gray–brown, developing dark, deep furrows, with light gray to white, scaly ridge tops

Leaf Color: Glossy, dark green

Fall Color: Russet red to red; sometimes outstanding

Flowers: Catkins

Fruit: Acorn

Disease & Insect Problems: None serious

Culture: Prefers moist well-drained soils; full sun; drought and high pH tolerant

Recommended Cultivars: None

Author Notes: This large, lowland shade tree is drought tolerant and readily transplantable. It is versatile with a growth habit, exhibits more dependable fall color than Pin and Scarlet Oaks, and is suitable for planting near streams. Shumard is one of the largest southern oaks.

Scientific Name: *Sassafras albidum*

Common Name: Common Sassafras

Hardiness Zones: 4–8

Mature Size: 30–60' tall x 25–40' wide

Habit: Pyramidal

Growth Rate: Medium–fast

Bark: Dark red–brown, with deep ridges and furrows

Leaf Color: Bright green, with distinctive "mitten" leaves; fragrant when crushed

Fall Color: Yellow–orange–red in October; spectacular

Flowers: Yellow in April before emerging leaves; ornamental

Fruit: Dark blue drupe in September on female plants

Disease & Insect Problems: Occasional bouts of iron chlorosis in high pH soils

Culture: Ideally suited in full sun for best autumn color but will tolerate partial shade; best in moist, loamy, acid, well-drained soil; prune in winter.

Recommended Cultivars: None

Author Notes: This attractive, medium-sized, native ornamental tree has spectacular autumn color. It makes a fine specimen or is excellent as a thicket in a naturalized setting. The Common Sassafras is found as single- or multi-trunked forms. It is practically impossible to transplant and thus must be container grown.

Scientific Name: *Stewartia pseudocamellia*

Common Name: Japanese Stewartia

Hardiness Zones: 5–7

Mature Size: 25–40' tall x 10–20' wide

Habit: Pyramidal

Growth Rate: Slow–medium

Bark: Camouflage-hued, exfoliated bark; flaky but smooth underneath in patches of gray, brown, and rust; outstanding

Leaf Color: Dark green and glabrous

Fall Color: Orange to red with occasional hues of red–purple

Flowers: Showy white in July; camellia-like, but tend to drop rather quickly

Fruit: Ovoid and pale green; not ornamental

Disease & Insect Problems: None serious

Culture: Full sun to partial shade; slightly acidic, moist, well-drained soil high in organic matter

Recommended Cultivars: None

Author Notes: One of the nicest multi-season ornamental trees for the garden, this stewartia offers magnificent peeling bark and fall color along with lovely white flowers in midsummer. Avoid placing this Japanese native in hot spots as it prefers morning sun. I find it performs best in light shade, especially in the hottest part of summer. It is a four-season plant.

Scientific Name: *Styrax japonicus*

Common Name: Japanese Snowbell

Hardiness Zones: 5–8

Mature Size: 20–30' tall & wide

Habit: Rounded, with low branching

Growth Rate: Medium

Bark: Handsome smooth gray–brown, with irregular orange–brown fissures

Leaf Color: Medium to dark green

Fall Color: Yellow to red; never sensational

Flowers: Bell-shaped white with yellow stamens in May to June on long pendulous stalks; slight fragrance; delicate yet beautiful

Fruit: Ovoid and gray; attractive in August–September

Disease & Insect Problems: None serious

Culture: Full sun to part shade; best in well-drained, moist, acid soil supplemented with organic matter

Recommended Cultivars:
'Emerald Pagoda': columnar habit, with larger flowers and robust leathery leaves
'Pendula': compact weeping form
'Pink Chimes': pink flowers; slight fragrance

Author Notes: This lovely, small, low-branched tree with a distinct horizontal appearance does well in and around patios. Another excellent, somewhat unknown, tree, the Japanese Snowbell has delicate white (or pink) flowers blooming in spring to early summer; it also has interesting bark. This tree may attract a significant number of bees when in bloom so be careful. It does not take heat well and requires supplemental watering. In cold climates, locate it in an area protected from winter winds.

Scientific Name: *Syringa pekinensis*

Common Names: Pekin Lilac
Peking Lilac
Chinese Tree Lilac

Hardiness Zones: 3–7

Mature Size: 15–20' tall x 10–15' wide

Habit: Oval

Growth Rate: Medium

Bark: Smooth and copper-colored with peeling and flaking in sheets; prominent horizontal lenticels add to the ornamental value

Leaf Color: Dark green and smooth

Fall Color: Dull yellow

Flowers: Fragrant creamy-white in long panicles during early summer

Fruit: Oblong and insignificant

Disease & Insect Problems: None serious, including powdery mildew

Culture: Full sun in well-drained soils; tolerant to drought and moist soils

Recommended Cultivars:
'Great Wall': upward sweeping branches create an upright oval form; sparkling white flowers
'Morton' (China Snow®): upright, with exfoliating cherry-like bark; single-stemmed
'Sun Dak' (Copper Curls®): coppery-orange exfoliating bark; multiple-trunked; improved winter hardiness

Author Notes: This is another small, tree-form lilac that can be used in the land-scape. Exhibiting greater heat tolerance than *S. reticulata*, the Pekin Lilac flowers earlier and has a finer texture because of its smaller leaves and stems. It can be grown as either a single-trunk or a multi-stemmed tree and exhibits a very nice winter feature of cherry-like bark.

Scientific Name: *Syringa reticulata*

Common Name: Japanese Tree Lilac

Hardiness Zones: 3–7

Mature Size: 20–30' tall x 15–25' wide

Habit: Upright oval, becoming rounded

Growth Rate: Medium

Bark: Red-brown; similar to cherry, with distinctive horizontal striping

Leaf Color: Dark green

Fall Color: Poor, like most lilacs

Flowers: Showy, creamy white panicles in early June; fragrant but not particularly pleasant

Fruit: Warty brown capsule, not ornamental

Disease & Insect Problems: None serious, including powdery mildew

Culture: Likes well-drained soil; pH adaptable; full sun for best flowering; prune after flowering

Recommended Cultivars:
'Ivory Silk': tight crown; heavy flowerer at young age
'Regent': upright; vigorous growth
'Summer Snow': rounded; flowers heavily

Author Notes: A small, tree-form lilac with showy, early-summer flowers, the Japanese Tree Lilac is considered an ornamental tree and best used as a specimen or street tree. It is the most trouble-free lilac available and can be found as single- or multi-trunked forms. It is also the most dependable lilac to plant for difficult sites.

Scientific Name: *Tilia cordata*

Common Name: Littleleaf Linden

Hardiness Zones: 3–7

Mature Size: 40–50' tall x 30' wide

Habit: Pyramidal in youth, becoming rounded oval with age

Growth Rate: Medium

Bark: Gray–brown in youth, becoming more rippled, furrowed, and darker

Leaf Color: Dark green, shiny, and heart-shaped

Fall Color: An uninspiring yellow–green to yellow

Flowers: Fragrant yellow–cream in late June to early July; attracts bees

Fruit: Small nutlet

Disease & Insect Problems: Some foliage damage may occur with Japanese beetles

Culture: Ideally suited in full sun; prefers moist, well-drained soil; pH adaptable

Recommended Cultivars:
  'Chancole' (Chancellor®): narrow and upright; lustrous, dark green leaves
  'Corzam' (Corinthian®): compact; great street tree
  'Greenspire': small whitish flowers; strong central leader; uniform branching

Author Notes: This large shade or specimen tree has a symmetrical shape, dense dark green foliage, and fragrant flowers in June to July. The Littleleaf Linden was initially thought to be more urban tolerant than it actually is. Common as a street tree in communities, it does not tolerate road salt well.

Scientific Name: *Tilia tomentosa*

Common Name: Silver Linden

Hardiness Zones: 4–7

Mature Size: 60' tall x 40' wide

Habit: Pyramidal in youth, becoming upright oval with age

Growth Rate: Medium

Bark: Light gray in youth (like beech), becoming gray–brown and furrowed

Leaf Color: Dark, glossy green on upper surface with silver lower surface

Fall Color: Yellow

Flowers: Fragrant yellow–white in late June to early July; attracts bees

Fruit: Small egg-shaped nutlet

Disease & Insect Problems: Some foliage damage may occur with Japanese beetles

Culture: Ideally suited in full sun; prefers moist, well-drained soil; pH adaptable; more urban tolerant than other lindens

Recommended Cultivar:

'Sterling', 'Sterling Silver': broad pyramid; foliage emerges silvery and retains the blue–silver undersides all season

Author Notes: A large pyramidal tree, the Silver Linden tolerates heat, drought, and pollution better than other lindens. This beautiful ornamental shade tree has light gray, smooth bark and bicolored leaves, dark green on top and shimmering silver beneath. It is a great choice for residential, parkland, and golf course settings.

Scientific Name: *Ulmus americana*

Common Name: American Elm

Hardiness Zones: 2–9

Mature Size: 70' tall x 40' wide

Habit: 3 distinct habits—vase-shape; oak-form; narrow-form

Growth Rate: Medium–fast

Bark: Dark gray with deep broad ridges

Leaf Color: Dark, glossy green, and lustrous

Fall Color: Typically yellow but variable

Flowers: Green–red in March; not showy

Fruit: Round samara in June; not ornamental

Disease & Insect Problems: Many, including Dutch elm disease, elm yellows (elm phloem necrosis), wetwood (bacterial), cankers

Culture: Prefers moist, rich soils but adaptable; full sun to partial shade; prune in fall

Recommended Cultivars:
'Jefferson': vase-shaped with arching branches; National Park Service introduction
'New Harmony': broad, vase-shaped; U.S. National Arboretum introduction
'Princeton': vase-shaped; fast grower; yellow fall color
'Valley Forge': classic American elm shape; most resistant of U.S. National Arboretum introductions; nice yellow fall color

Author Notes: At one time used extensively as a street and large shade tree before the onslaught of Dutch elm disease, the American Elm should now be planted only in the Dutch elm disease-resistant (tolerant) cultivars listed above. This elm has a majestic character (including its famous vase-shaped form) that is very unique and graceful.

Scientific Name: *Ulmus parviflora*

Common Names: Lacebark Elm
Chinese Elm

Hardiness Zones: 5–9

Mature Size: 40–50' tall & wide

Habit: Upright oval, becoming rounded

Growth Rate: Medium

Bark: A magnificent mottled and exfoliating combination of green, gray, orange, and brown

Leaf Color: Shiny, dark green, and serrated

Fall Color: Yellow–red–purple in early to mid-November

Flowers: Inconspicuous in August to September

Fruit: Samara; lime green initially, turning a deep red

Disease & Insect Problems: None serious

Culture: Adaptable to extremes of soil and pH; prefers moist, well-drained, fertile soils; shows excellent urban tolerance; full sun to partial sun

Recommended Cultivars:
'BSNUPF' (Everclear®): upright, columnar form
'Emerald Isle', 'Emer I' (Athena®): rounded; may be hardiest selection
'Emerald Vase', 'Emer II' (Allee®): upright, vase-shaped; smaller form of American elm
'Ohio': USNA introduction with reddish fall color
'Small Frye': selection by plant guru Michael Dirr; small tree with a mushroom top

Author Notes: A durable large shade, street, or specimen tree. Arguably the best all-around elm because of its combination of foliage, fall color, ornamental bark, and resistance to Dutch elm disease. Branch strength of this tree is sometimes questioned as ice and windstorms may cause damage.

Scientific Name: *Ulmus x Frontier*

Common Name: Frontier Elm

Hardiness Zones: 5–8

Mature Size: 40' tall x 30' wide

Habit: Oval

Growth Rate: Medium–fast

Bark: Smooth gray–green with orange lenticels

Leaf Color: Dark green, glossy, and lustrous

Fall Color: Red–purple–burgundy

Flowers: Rarely

Fruit: None

Disease & Insect Problems: Hybrid elm exhibits both a high level of disease tolerance to Dutch elm disease, phloem necrosis, and moderate resistance to the elm leaf beetle

Culture: Prefers moist, rich soils but adaptable to poor soils; full sun; very tolerant of urban conditions and drought tolerant

Recommended Cultivars: N/A

Author Notes: This promising elm is now available. A cross between *U. carpinifolia* (Smooth) and *U. parviflora* (Lacebark) Elms, this exciting, medium-sized tree may be blazing a trail for elms in the urban landscape. It has good vigor, tolerates poor soils, grows fast but does not get big, has small leaves and no seeds, is resistant of insect and disease problems, and has outstanding long fall color. The Frontier Elm should be on everyone's street-tree list.

Scientific Name: *Zelkova serrata*

Common Name: Japanese Zelkova

Hardiness Zones: 5–8

Mature Size: 60' tall & wide

Habit: Upright vase

Growth Rate: Medium–fast

Bark: Red–brown, cherry-like in youth; gray–brown, with some exfoliation at maturity

Leaf Color: Dark green and serrated

Fall Color: Yellow–orange–brown, with occasional hues of red–purple

Flowers: Not showy in April with leaves

Fruit: Kidney bean-shaped drupe ripening in October hidden by foliage; not showy

Disease & Insect Problems: None serious

Culture: Prefers moist, deep well-drained soils; adaptable and shows excellent urban tolerance to heat, drought, poor soils, and varying pH; full sun to partial sun

Recommended Cultivars:
   'Green Vase': vase-shaped; vigorous with upward-arching branches
   'Musashino': upright, columnar-vase-shaped; yellow fall color
   'Ogon': yellow spring leaves turning yellow–green by midsummer; stems remain
      amber gold and are striking in winter
   'Village Green': oval; wine–red fall color

Author Notes: This handsome large shade tree offers a vase shape, rapid growth, and stately looks. Its other ornamental assets include its foliage, fine texture, and attractive bark. This is really an underutilized tree selection in today's landscapes, parks, and golf courses. It is also very tolerant of pollution and city conditions.

Scientific Name: *Abies balsamea* var. *phanerolepis*

Common Name: Canaan Fir

Hardiness Zones: 3–8

Mature Size: 40' tall x 20–30' wide

Habit: Pyramidal

Growth Rate: Fast

Bark: Smooth and thin in youth, becoming thicker and more furrowed

Leaf Color: Evergreen; deep rich green, with a soft texture

Fall Color: N/A

Flowers: Inconspicuous

Fruit: Cone

Disease & Insect Problems: None serious but the Balsam wooly adelgid is a small, wingless insect to monitor

Culture: Ideally suited in full sun to partial shade; prefers slightly acid, well-drained soil but has performed well in heavier (clay) soil

Recommended Cultivars: None

Author Notes: One of the top and most popular Christmas-tree types, this fir is heat, humidity, and drought tolerant. This medium-sized tree will grow in areas not suited for other firs. It also tolerates moist sites and late frosts. The Canaan is a strong candidate to be used more in landscape settings.

Scientific Name: *Abies concolor*

Common Names: White Fir
Concolor Fir

Hardiness Zones: 3–7

Mature Size: 40' tall x 15–20' wide

Habit: Pyramidal

Growth Rate: Slow–medium

Bark: Smooth and thin in youth, becoming thicker and more furrowed; gray

Leaf Color: Evergreen; blue–gray–green soft foliage

Fall Color: N/A

Flowers: Inconspicuous

Fruit: Cone about 5" long, pale green initially, then maturing to deep purple and, finally, brown; ornamental

Disease & Insect Problems: None serious

Culture: Full sun to partial shade; prefers moist, rich, well-drained, gravelly soil; adaptable to poor soils but not to heavy clay soil

Recommended Cultivars:
'Blue Cloak': powder blue needles, especially on new growth; slight weeping habit
'Candicans': blue–white needles make for a real focal point; narrow form

Author Notes: This is one of the best firs for the Midwest (along with Canaan) in terms of drought, heat tolerance, and cold. A stately, slow-growing, soft-needled evergreen with a blue–silver cast, it is best used as a specimen tree. An excellent Christmas and ornamental tree, the Concolor is known as the most beautiful of the firs.

Scientific Name: *Juniperus virginiana*

Common Name: Eastern Redcedar

Hardiness Zones: 3–9

Mature Size: 40–50' tall x 8–20' wide

Habit: Pyramidal

Growth Rate: Medium

Bark: Gray–red–brown, with some exfoliation in long strips

Leaf Color: Evergreen; green to blue-green

Fall Color: N/A

Flowers: Somewhat interesting in late winter; yellow–brown

Fruit: Cone

Disease & Insect Problems: Cedar-apple rust and bagworms

Culture: Extremely adaptable to varying adverse conditions, soil types, and pH levels; seems to thrive in limestone-based soil; full sun

Recommended Cultivars:
'Burkii': pyramidal; 10–25' tall; gray-blue, with purple cast in winter
'Emerald Sentinel': columnar; 20' tall x 8' wide; dark green foliage
'Grey Owl': compact and spreading; 3' tall x 7' wide; shrubby, and a substitute for Pfitzer Juniper; silver-gray

Author Notes: This medium-sized juniper is best utilized in group plantings for screens, windbreaks, or hedges. It is a very durable and tolerant evergreen for which cultivars should be sought out in preference over the species as the species will quickly naturalize in unmaintained land areas.

Scientific Name: *Metasequoia glyptostroboides*

Common Name: Dawn Redwood

Hardiness Zones: 5–8

Mature Size: 70' tall x 25' wide

Habit: Conical

Growth Rate: Medium–fast

Bark: Red–brown in youth, becoming darker, fissured, and exfoliating in narrow strips

Leaf Color: Deciduous; bright green

Fall Color: Cinnamon brown

Flowers: Inconspicuous

Fruit: Cone

Disease & Insect Problems: None serious

Culture: Does best in moist, deep, well-drained, slightly acid soil; full sun; does not tolerate high pH soil but seems to adapt to heavy (clay) soil

Recommended Cultivars:
'Miss Grace': weeping form and slow growing; blue-green foliage
'Ogon', 'Gold Rush': yellow leaves; burnt orange fall color; fast grower
'Raven' (Shaw's Legacy®): uniform pyramidal shape; dark green needles; deep furrowed bark
'Snow Flurry': spotted form with whitish color on tips of needles

Author Notes: This large, stately, deciduous conifer exhibits a distinct conical form. It is a lovely specimen and ornamental tree excelling in groves, and along streams and lakes. Plant it in areas large enough to accommodate its size like parks and golf courses. It also makes a very effective screen.

Scientific Name: *Picea omorika*

Common Name: Serbian Spruce

Hardiness Zones: 4–7

Mature Size: 50' tall x 20' wide

Habit: Pyramidal

Growth Rate: Slow–medium

Bark: Mocha brown, thin, and scaly plates

Leaf Color: Evergreen; glossy, dark green

Fall Color: N/A

Flowers: Long and attractive, with a pink–red hue

Fruit: Cone

Disease & Insect Problems: Bagworms, borers, budworms, and spider mites, but none serious

Culture: Best in a deep, rich soil that is moist and well-drained; pH adaptable; best in partial shade, but tolerable to full sun; best to offer some protection from strong winter winds

Recommended Cultivars:
'Nana': dwarf; dense and globular in youth; becomes a broad pyramid
'Pendula Bruns': very strong weeping form

Author Notes: A beautiful, large, evergreen specimen tree noted for its narrow, pyramidal silhouette. Graceful, arching branches add to its merits. It is useful as a specimen, screen, or in groups. Here is a spruce that should be recognized and used more in the landscape but it needs some protection from winter winds.

Scientific Name: *Picea orientalis*

Common Name: Oriental Spruce

Hardiness Zones: 4–7

Mature Size: 55' tall x 20' wide

Habit: Pyramidal

Growth Rate: Slow

Bark: Brown, with some exfoliation in thin scales

Leaf Color: Evergreen; glossy, dark green

Fall Color: N/A

Flowers: Attractive with a red hue

Fruit: Cone; reddish in youth

Disease & Insect Problems: Mites, aphids, and bagworms, but none serious

Culture: Will tolerate poor and clay soil, but should be well-drained; pH adaptable; partial shade to full sun; best to offer some protection from harsh winter winds; sheltered locations offer the best sites

Recommended Cultivars:
'Gowdy': narrow form; 8–10' tall x 4–5' wide; pink cones
'Nana': dwarf form; < 3' tall
'Skylands': pyramidal; golden yellow-tipped needles

Author Notes: This extremely attractive, large, evergreen specimen tree is noted for its dense, narrow, pyramidal habit with pendulous, horizontal branching. Here is another spruce that needs to be more readily available for use in the landscape but requires some protection from winter winds.

Scientific Name: *Pinus bungeana*

Common Name: Lacebark Pine

Hardiness Zones: 4–7

Mature Size: 30–40' tall x 20–30' wide

Habit: Pyramidal–rounded

Growth Rate: Slow . . . have patience

Bark: Exfoliating in patches of green, white, gray, orange, and brown; handsome

Leaf Color: Evergreen; lustrous medium to dark green

Fall Color: N/A

Flowers: Inconspicuous

Fruit: Cone

Disease & Insect Problems: None serious

Culture: Requires well-drained soil; full sun; will tolerate slightly alkaline soils

Recommended Cultivars:
  'Great Wall': columnar with broad form; high density of needles and branches
  'Rowe Arboretum': exhibits more compact, uniform growth habit

Author Notes: This excellent, medium-sized, four-season specimen tree is valued for its showy, striking bark. It must be steadily limbed-up from a young age in order for its trunk and larger branches to receive the proper sunlight necessary to develop the mottled bark appearance. Beware that some damage may occur under heavy snowfall and ice loads on multi-trunked forms.

Scientific Name: *Pinus strobus*

Common Name: Eastern White Pine

Hardiness Zones: 3–7

Mature Size: 50–70' tall x 20–35' wide

Habit: Pyramidal in youth, becoming spreading

Growth Rate: Fast

Bark: Thin, smooth, gray–green in youth; darker and deeply furrowed with age

Leaf Color: Evergreen; blue-green to medium green and soft texture

Fall Color: N/A

Flowers: Inconspicuous

Fruit: Cone

Disease & Insect Problems: White Pine blister rust and White Pine weevil

Culture: Ideally suited in moist, well-drained, acid soil but somewhat adaptable; full sun to partial shade

Recommended Cultivars:
'Angel Falls': fine-textured columnar; graceful weeping branches
'Golden Candles': dwarf with brilliant yellow spring growth, turning to a soft green
'Fastigiata': narrow, upright-vase columnar
'Pendula': irregular twisting, droopy, weeping form

Author Notes: This handsome large specimen or shade tree also makes (in group plantings) a superb windbreak or screen. Seasonal yellowing occurs on older needles during autumn, but that is normal and not indicative of any problems. Chlorosis may develop in high pH, clay soils. This pine is susceptible to winter salt spray (do not plant near roadways) and to strong storms which can cause broken branches.

Scientific Name: *Taxodium distichum*

Common Name: Common Baldcypress

Hardiness Zones: 4–9

Mature Size: 50–70' tall x 20–30' wide

Habit: Pyramidal

Growth Rate: Medium

Bark: Red–brown and ornamentally attractive, with some exfoliation

Leaf Color: Deciduous; bright yellow green in spring; sage green in summer

Fall Color: Russet–orange–bronze

Flowers: Pendulous 4" long panicles, but considered ornamentally insignificant

Fruit: Cone

Disease & Insect Problems: None serious

Culture: Prefers acid, sandy soil with abundant moisture in the surface layers; adaptable to very dry or very wet sites and heavy, alkaline soil; full sun

Recommended Cultivars:
 'Cascade Falls': dwarf weeping; 8–12' tall at maturity; slow growing
 'Michelson' (Shawnee Brave™): narrow, fastigiate form; blue–green foliage
 'Peve Minaret': dwarf pyramidal form; 8–10' tall x 3' wide; compact with fat trunk

Author Notes: This large, deciduous conifer is an upright, stately, pyramidal tree. Use as a focal point or specimen. It is superb in exceptionally moist areas where the infamous "knees" form if roots are submerged. Versatile, it is also dry-site capable. Some chlorosis may occur in high pH soils.

Signs and Symptoms of EAB

Epicormic sprouts from trunk

Adult beetle

Serpentine frass-filled galleries

Flat, tapeworm-like larva

Woodpecker activity

Thinning canopy

D-shaped exit holes in bark

Emerald Ash Borer

EAB

As you may have noticed, there are no selections of ash (*Fraxinus* spp.) trees mentioned or recommended. The estimated 8 billion ash trees across the United States seem doomed—likely destroyed by the tiny, voracious emerald ash borer. Planting any ash species currently poses a risk.

The emerald ash borer is a selective pest that was brought into the United States (Detroit area) from China via wooden packing crates (pallets) in 2002. This beetle is not a threat to healthy Asian ash trees but is wreaking havoc to millions of ash trees in the Midwest. In fact all 16 native ash species are at risk of infestation, including their cultivars.

The native ash species make up 6 percent of our nation's forests. Ash trees common in the landscape—the green ash (*F. pennsylvanica*) and the white ash (*F. americana*)—have been planted as landscape, street, and park trees in great numbers. They transplant easily, are fast growing, and are very tolerant of urban growing conditions and sites. Sadly, some of these trees were replanted to replace the American elm trees lost to Dutch elm disease. They provide shade and a statuesque appearance to any landscape.

Adult borers are bright emerald green with dark undersides and are very small, averaging 0.5 inch in length. They breed within a week of emergence from ⅛" diameter, D-shaped, exit holes on the main trunk and branches. The females lay approximately 75 eggs in bark crevices in the upper third of the tree during midsummer. There the insect often remains undetected until symptoms appear. Within a week, the eggs hatch and larvae immediately begin their serpentine tunneling just beneath the cork cambium. They feed on phloem (food-conducting) and some xylem (water-conducting) tissue. As the larvae grow, so do the problems. Feeding continues until the arrival of cold temperatures when the larvae overwinter in a dormant mode. Pupation then begins the following April, continuing through early June, with adult beetles emerging about two weeks after the start of pupation. Males live 10 to 14 days while females live 21 days.

Larval feeding causes almost all of the injuries. The serpentine pattern of feeding can effectively girdle a branch in a single season. Most trees afflicted die because of the girdling. Symptoms of an infestation begin with chlorotic, unhealthy foliage, followed by canopy decline and branch dieback. This usually occurs in the upper third of the crown. Trees often die within three to five years of the initial egg laying.

Humans are a significant vector of EAB by transporting infested firewood to uninfested areas. A few control measures include using the systemic insecticide imidacloprid (Merit®/Xytect™) by soil drenching or injection or using emamectin benzoate (TREE-ãge™) by trunk injection during the spring. Cost of such treatments is expensive, ranging from $100–$300 dependent on tree size. Dinotefuran (Safari™) is relatively new and more expensive, but it offers control as a systemic bark spray. Studies show that a combination of larval and adult control will help slow the spread of infestation.

Biological controls such as parasitic moths or wasps may one day be a viable alternative. Scientists are also working on a hybrid North American/Asian ash tree.

A great lesson learned through this unfortunate infestation is that the loss of a particular genus from overplanting practices often will have a negative scenic impact on the landscape both in woodlots and around cities. It is always prudent to plant a variety of trees to lessen any impact that could be caused by disease or insects.

For the latest information on the status of EAB, please visit www .emeraldashborer.info. To preserve the American ash, early detection is the key. One has to be able to identify the emerald ash borer and the symptoms of its damage. If an infestation is detected, swift action is required to attempt to eradicate the pesky beetle. If you suspect or see any presence of EAB, immediately report the discovery to local and/or state authorities.

Plant Usage Guide

Scientific Name

Trees Considered Small-Sized

Acer buergerianum

Acer griseum

Acer pensylvanicum

Aesculus parviflora

Aesculus pavia

Amelanchier spp.

Asimina triloba

Carpinus caroliniana

Cercis canadensis

Chionanthus virginicus

Cornus alternifolia

Cornus florida

Cornus kousa

Cornus mas

Franklinia alatamaha

Halesia carolina

Heptacodium miconioides

Magnolia stellata

Magnolia virginiana

Malus spp.

Parrotia persica

Styrax japonicus

Syringa pekinensis

Syringa reticulata

Trees Considered Medium-Sized

Abies balsamea var. phanerolepis

Abies concolor

Acer rubrum

Carpinus betulus

Cercidiphyllum japonicum

Cladrastis kentukea

Juniperus virginiana

Koelreuteria paniculata

Ostrya virginiana

Oxydendrum arboreum

Pinus bungeana

Sassafras albidum

Stewartia pseudocamellia

Ulmus x Frontier

Trees Considered Large-Sized

Acer saccharum

Aesculus octandra

Betula nigra

Fagus sylvatica

Ginkgo biloba

Gleditsia triacanthos var. inermis

Gymnocladus dioicus

Liriodendron tulipifera
Magnolia acuminata
Metasequoia glyptostroboides
Nyssa sylvatica
Picea omorika
Picea orientalis
Pinus strobus
Quercus acutissima
Quercus bicolor
Quercus imbricaria
Quercus muehlenbergii
Quercus palustris
Quercus rubra
Quercus shumardii
Taxodium distichum
Tilia cordata
Tilia tomentosa
Ulmus americana
Ulmus parviflora
Zelkova serrata

Trees for Dry Areas

Abies balsamea var. phanerolepis
Cladrastis kentukea
Ginkgo biloba
Gleditsia triacanthos var. inermis
Juniperus virginiana
Koelreuteria paniculata
Malus spp.
Pinus strobus
Quercus imbricaria
Quercus muehlenbergii
Quercus rubra
Syringa pekinensis
Tilia tomentosa

Trees for Wet Areas*

Acer rubrum
Amelanchier spp.
Betula nigra
Carpinus caroliniana
Gleditsia triacanthos var. inermis
Magnolia virginiana
Metasequoia glyptostroboides
Nyssa sylvatica
Quercus bicolor
Quercus palustris
Quercus shumardii
Taxodium distichum
Tilia tomentosa
Ulmus americana

Trees for Four–Season Appeal

Acer griseum
Amelanchier spp.
Betula nigra
Cornus florida
Cornus kousa
Fagus sylvatica
Parrotia persica
Pinus bungeana
Stewartia pseudocamellia

Trees for Spring Flowers

Aesculus octandra
Aesculus pavia
Amelanchier spp.
Cercis canadensis
Chionanthus virginicus
Cladrastis kentukea

*Generally suited for areas prone to occasional flooding and/or ponding of water such as stream banks, low areas, etc.

Cornus alternifolia
Cornus florida
Cornus kousa
Cornus mas
Halesia carolina
Liriodendron tulipifera
Magnolia acuminata
Magnolia stellata
Malus spp.
Sassafras albidum
Styrax japonicus

Trees for Summer Flowers

Aesculus parviflora
Franklinia alatamaha
Heptacodium miconioides
Koelreuteria paniculata
Magnolia virginiana
Oxydendrum arboreum
Stewartia pseudocamellia
Syringa pekinensis
Syringa reticulata
Tilia cordata
Tilia tomentosa

Trees for Fall Color

Acer buergerianum
Acer griseum
Acer pensylvanicum
Acer rubrum
Acer saccharum
Aesculus octandra
Amelanchier spp.
Asimina triloba
Betula nigra
Carpinus caroliniana

Cercidiphyllum japonicum
Cladrastis kentukea
Cornus florida
Cornus kousa
Franklinia alatamaha
Ginkgo biloba
Gleditsia triacanthos var. inermis
Liriodendron tulipifera
Magnolia acuminata
Metasequoia glyptostroboides
Nyssa sylvatica
Oxydendrum arboreum
Parrotia persica
Quercus palustris
Quercus shumardii
Sassafras albidum
Stewartia pseudocamellia
Taxodium distichum
Ulmus parviflora
Ulmus x Frontier

Trees for Winter Interest

Abies concolor (texture)
Acer buergerianum (bark)
Acer griseum (bark)
Acer pensylvanicum (bark)
Amelanchier spp. (bark)
Betulus nigra (bark)
Carpinus caroliniana (bark)
Fagus sylvatica (bark)
Gymnocladus dioicus (texture)
Malus spp. (fruit)
Oxydendrum arboreum (bark)
Pinus bungeana (bark)
Quercus bicolor (texture)
Stewartia pseudocamellia (bark)
Syringa pekinensis (bark)

Trees for Ornamental Bark

Acer buergerianum
Acer griseum
Acer pensylvanicum
Amelanchier spp.
Betula nigra
Carpinus betulus
Fagus sylvatica
Heptacodium miconioides
Metasequoia glyptostroboides
Parrotia persica
Pinus bungeana
Stewartia pseudocamellia
Taxodium distichum
Ulmus parviflora
Zelkova serrata

Trees Considered to be Ornamental*

Acer griseum
Amelanchier spp.
Cercis canadensis
Cladrastis kentukea
Cornus kousa
Cornus mas
Franklinia alatamaha
Halesia carolina
Heptacodium miconioides
Koelreuteria paniculata
Magnolia stellata
Magnolia virginiana
Malus spp.
Parrotia persica
Stewartia pseudocamellia
Syringa pekinensis
Syringa reticulata

Trees with Ornamental Fruit

Amelanchier spp.
Asimina triloba
Chionanthus virginicus
Cornus alternifolia
Cornus florida
Cornus kousa
Cornus mas
Heptacodium miconioides
Magnolia acuminata
Magnolia virginiana
Malus spp.
Nyssa sylvatica
Sassafras albidum

Trees Considered to be Specimens

Abies concolor
Acer griseum
Acer rubrum (cultivars)
Aesculus pavia
Amelanchier spp.
Cercidiphyllum japonicum
Chionanthus virginicus
Cornus florida
Cornus kousa
Cornus mas
Fagus sylvatica
Franklinia alatamaha
Ginkgo biloba
Magnolia stellata
Malus spp.
Metasequoia glyptostroboides
Nyssa sylvatica
Oxydendrum arboreum
Parrotia persica

*Generally considered ornamental if under 30' and having one or more ornamental aspects.

Picea omorika
Picea orientalis
Pinus bungeana
Pinus strobus
Quercus muehlenbergii
Sassafras albidum
Stewartia pseudocamellia
Styrax japonicus
Syringa pekinensis
Syringa reticulata
Taxodium distichum
Tilia cordata
Ulmus parviflora

Trees Tolerant of Partial Shade

Acer pensylvanicum
Aesculus parviflora
Amelanchier spp.
Asimina triloba
Carpinus caroliniana
Cercis canadensis
Chionanthus virginicus
Cornus alternifolia
Cornus florida
Cornus mas
Halesia carolina
Magnolia virginiana
Ostrya virginiana
Parrotia persica
Picea omorika
Picea orientalis
Sassafras albidum
Stewartia pseudocamellia
Styrax japonicus

Trees for Shade Effect

Acer buergerianum
Acer rubrum
Acer saccharum
Aesculus octandra
Betula nigra
Fagus sylvatica
Ginkgo biloba
Koelreuteria paniculata
Magnolia acuminata
Nyssa sylvatica
Pinus strobus
Quercus acutissima
Quercus imbricaria
Quercus palustris
Quercus rubra
Quercus shumardii
Tilia cordata
Tilia tomentosa
Ulmus umericana
Zelkova serrata

Trees Tolerant of Salt Spray

Amelanchier spp.
Gleditsia triacanthos var. *inermis*
Juniperus virginiana
Nyssa sylvatica
Tilia cordata

Trees for Screens

Abies concolor
Amelanchier spp.
Asimina triloba
Carpinus betulus
Carpinus caroliniana

Cornus mas
Juniperus virginiana
Metasequoia glyptostroboides
Picea omorika
Pinus strobus
Sassafras albidum

Trees for Urban Settings

Carpinus betulus
Gingko biloba
Gleditsia triacanthos var. inermis
Juniperus virginiana
Koelreuteria paniculata
Parrotia persica
Quercus palustris
Quercus rubra
Tilia tomentosa
Ulmus parviflora
Ulmus x Frontier
Zelkova serrata

Trees Tolerant of High pH Soils

Acer griseum
Acer saccharum

Aesculus parviflora
Aesculus pavia
Amelanchier spp.
Carpinus betulus
Cercidiphyllum japonicum
Cercis canadensis
Cladrastis kentukea
Cornus mas
Ginkgo biloba
Gleditsia triacanthos var. inermis
Gymnocladus dioicus
Heptacodium miconioides
Juniperus virginiana
Koelreuteria paniculata
Magnolia acuminata
Magnolia stellata
Malus spp.
Parrotia persica
Quercus muehlenbergii
Syringa pekinensis
Syringa reticulata
Taxodium distichum
Tilia cordata
Tilia tomentosa
Ulmus x Frontier

Plant Usage Guide

Common Name

Trees Considered Small-Sized

American Hornbeam
Bottlebrush Buckeye
Carolina Silverbell
Common Pawpaw
Cornelian Cherry Dogwood
Eastern Redbud
Flowering Crabapple
Flowering Dogwood
Franklinia
Japanese Snowbell
Japanese Tree Lilac
Kousa Dogwood
Pagoda Dogwood
Paperbark Maple
Pekin Lilac
Persian Parrotia
Red Buckeye
Seven-son Flower
Serviceberry
Star Magnolia
Striped Maple
Sweetbay Magnolia
Trident Maple
White Fringetree

Trees Considered Medium-Sized

American Hophornbeam
American Yellowwood
Canaan Fir
Common Sassafras
Eastern Redcedar
European Hornbeam
Frontier Elm
Japanese Stewartia
Katsuratree
Lacebark Pine
Panicled Goldenraintree
Red Maple
Sourwood
White Fir

Trees Considered Large-Sized

American Elm
Black Tupelo
Chinkapin Oak
Common Baldcypress
Cucumbertree Magnolia
Dawn Redwood
Eastern White Pine

European Beech
Ginkgo
Japanese Zelkova
Kentucky Coffeetree
Lacebark Elm
Littleleaf Linden
Oriental Spruce
Pin Oak
Red Oak
River Birch
Sawtooth Oak
Serbian Spruce
Shingle Oak
Shumard Oak
Silver Linden
Sugar Maple
Swamp White Oak
Thornless Honeylocust
Tuliptree
Yellow Buckeye

Trees for Dry Areas

American Yellowwood
Canaan Fir
Chinkapin Oak
Eastern Redcedar
Eastern White Pine
Flowering Crabapple
Ginkgo
Panicled Goldenraintree
Pekin Lilac
Red Oak
Shingle Oak
Silver Linden
Thornless Honeylocust

Trees for Wet Areas*

American Elm
American Hornbeam
Black Tupelo
Common Baldcypress
Dawn Redwood
Pin Oak
Red Maple
River Birch
Serviceberry
Shumard Oak
Silver Linden
Swamp White Oak
Sweetbay Magnolia
Thornless Honeylocust

Trees for Four-Season Appeal

European Beech
Flowering Dogwood
Japanese Stewartia
Kousa Dogwood
Lacebark Pine
Paperbark Maple
Persian Parrotia
River Birch
Serviceberry

Trees for Spring Flowers

American Yellowwood
Carolina Silverbell
Common Sassafras
Cornelian Cherry Dogwood
Cucumbertree Magnolia
Eastern Redbud

*Generally suited for areas prone to occasional flooding and/or ponding of water such as stream banks, low areas, etc.

Flowering Crabapple
Flowering Dogwood
Japanese Snowbell
Kousa Dogwood
Pagoda Dogwood
Red Buckeye
Serviceberry
Star Magnolia
Tuliptree
White Fringetree
Yellow Buckeye

Trees for Summer Flowers

Bottlebrush Buckeye
Franklinia
Japanese Stewartia
Japanese Tree Lilac
Littleleaf Linden
Panicled Goldenraintree
Pekin Lilac
Seven-son Flower
Silver Linden
Sourwood
Sweetbay Magnolia

Trees for Fall Color

American Hornbeam
American Yellowwood
Black Tupelo
Common Baldcypress
Common Pawpaw
Common Sassafras
Cucumbertree Magnolia
Dawn Redwood
Flowering Dogwood
Franklinia

Frontier Elm
Ginkgo
Japanese Stewartia
Katsuratree
Kousa Dogwood
Lacebark Elm
Paperbark Maple
Persian Parrotia
Pin Oak
Red Maple
River Birch
Serviceberry
Shumard Oak
Sourwood
Striped Maple
Sugar Maple
Thornless Honeylocust
Trident Maple
Tuliptree
Yellow Buckeye

Trees for Winter Interest

American Hornbeam (bark)
European Beech (bark)
Flowering Crabapple (fruit)
Japanese Stewartia (bark)
Kentucky Coffeetree (texture)
Lacebark Pine (bark)
Paperbark Maple (bark)
Pekin Lilac (bark)
River Birch (bark)
Serviceberry (bark)
Sourwood (bark)
Striped Maple (bark)
Swamp White Oak (texture)
Trident Maple (bark)
White Fir (texture)

Trees for Ornamental Bark

Common Baldcypress
Dawn Redwood
European Beech
European Hornbeam
Japanese Stewartia
Japanese Zelkova
Lacebark Elm
Lacebark Pine
Paperbark Maple
Persian Parrotia
River Birch
Serviceberry
Seven-son Flower
Striped Maple
Trident Maple

Trees with Ornamental Fruit

Black Tupelo
Common Pawpaw
Common Sassafras
Corneliancherry Dogwood
Cucumbertree Magnolia
Flowering Crabapple
Flowering Dogwood
Kousa Dogwood
Pagoda Dogwood
Serviceberry
Seven-son Flower
Sweetbay Magnolia
White Fringetree

Trees Considered to be Ornamental*

American Yellowwood
Carolina Silverbell
Corneliancherry Dogwood
Eastern Redbud
Flowering Crabapple
Franklinia
Japanese Stewartia
Japanese Tree Lilac
Kousa Dogwood
Panicled Goldenraintree
Paperbark Maple
Pekin Lilac
Persian Parrotia
Serviceberry
Seven-son Flower
Star Magnolia
Sweetbay Magnolia

Trees Considered to be Specimens

Black Tupelo
Chinkapin Oak
Common Baldcypress
Common Sassafras
Corneliancherry Dogwood
Dawn Redwood
Eastern White Pine
European Beech
Flowering Crabapple
Flowering Dogwood
Franklinia
Ginkgo
Japanese Snowbell
Japanese Stewartia
Japanese Tree Lilac
Katsuratree
Kousa Dogwood
Lacebark Elm
Lacebark Pine

*Generally considered ornamental if under 30' and having one or more ornamental aspects.

Littleleaf Linden
Oriental Spruce
Paperbark Maple
Pekin Lilac
Persian Parrotia
Red Buckeye
Red Maple (cultivars)
Serbian Spruce
Serviceberry
Sourwood
Star Magnolia
White Fir
White Fringetree

Trees Tolerant of Partial Shade

American Hophornbeam
American Hornbeam
Bottlebrush Buckeye
Carolina Silverbell
Common Pawpaw
Common Sassafras
Corneliancherry Dogwood
Eastern Redbud
Flowering Dogwood
Japanese Snowbell
Japanese Stewartia
Oriental Spruce
Pagoda Dogwood
Persian Parrotia
Serbian Spruce
Serviceberry
Striped Maple
Sweetbay Magnolia
White Fringetree

Trees for Shade Effect

American Elm
Black Tupelo
Cucumbertree Magnolia
Eastern White Pine
European Beech
Ginkgo
Japanese Zelkova
Littleleaf Linden
Panicled Goldenraintree
Pin Oak
Red Maple
Red Oak
River Birch
Sawtooth Oak
Shingle Oak
Shumard Oak
Silver Linden
Sugar Maple
Trident Maple
Yellow Buckeye

Trees Tolerant of Salt Spray

Black Tupelo
Eastern Redcedar
Thornless Honeylocust
Littleleaf Linden
Serviceberry

Trees for Screens

American Hornbeam
Common Pawpaw
Common Sassafras
Corneliancherry Dogwood
Dawn Redwood

Eastern Redcedar
Eastern White Pine
European Hornbeam
Serbian Spruce
Serviceberry
White Fir

Trees for Urban Settings

Eastern Redcedar
European Hornbeam
Frontier Elm
Ginkgo
Japanese Zelkova
Lacebark Elm
Panicled Goldenraintree
Persian Parrotia
Pin Oak
Red Oak
Silver Linden
Thornless Honeylocust

Trees Tolerant of High pH Soils

American Yellowwood
Bottlebrush Buckeye

Chinkapin Oak
Common Baldcypress
Corneliancherry Dogwood
Cucumbertree Magnolia
Eastern Redbud
Eastern Redcedar
European Hornbeam
Flowering Crabapple
Frontier Elm
Ginkgo
Japanese Tree Lilac
Katsuratree
Kentucky Coffeetree
Littleleaf Linden
Panicled Goldenraintree
Paperbark Maple
Pekin Lilac
Persian Parrotia
Red Buckeye
Serviceberry
Seven-son Flower
Silver Linden
Star Magnolia
Sugar Maple
Thornless Honeylocust

Bibliography

Books

Dirr, Michael A. *Dirr's Encyclopedia of Trees and Shrubs.* Portland, OR: Timber Press, Inc., 2011.

———. *Manual of Woody Landscape Plants: Their Identification, Ornamental Characteristics, Culture, Propagation, and Uses*, 5th ed. Champaign, IL: Stipes Publishing, 1998.

Hurdzan, Michael J. *Golf Course Architecture: Design, Construction, and Restoration*. Ann Arbor, MI: Sleeping Bear Press, 1996.

Lilly, Sharon. *Golf Course Tree Management.* Ann Arbor, MI: Sleeping Bear Press, 1999.

Sydnor, T. Davis, Randall Heiligmann, and Keith L. Smith. *Ash Replacements for Urban and Woodland Plantings*. Bulletin 924. Columbus, OH: The Ohio State University Extension, 2005.

——— and William F. Cowen. *Ohio Trees*. Bulletin 700. Columbus, OH: The Ohio State University Extension, 2000.

Magazines

American Gardener
Backyard Living
Fine Gardening
Golf Journal
Horticulture
Tree Services
Turf (formerly *Turf Central*)

Newspaper

Columbus Dispatch

Websites

ArborCom. http://www.arborcom.ca.
Arbor Day Foundation. http://www.arborday.org.

Golf Course Superintendents Association of America. http://www.gcsaa.org.

Ohio State University Plantfacts. http://www.plantfacts.osu.edu.

University of Connecticut Plant Database. http://www.hort.uconn.edu/plants.

United States Golf Association. http://www.usga.org.

Index

Scientific names are displayed in italicized type.
Common names are displayed in roman type.
Numbers in italics indicate those pages with photographs.

About the Author

AN ACCOMPLISHED AND longtime gardener, **Scott Zanon** holds a bachelor of science degree in both agronomy (turfgrass science) and horticulture (landscape horticulture) from The Ohio State University. In 2009, his first book, *Desirable Trees for the Midwest: 50 for the Home Landscape and Larger Properties*, was well received in the trade due to its user-friendly style. His magazine articles have been published in *State-by-State Gardening*. Zanon has spoken many times to garden clubs, master gardeners, and students in the Ohio State University Nursery Short Course, and has been a guest on the nationally syndicated talk radio program "In the Garden with Ron Wilson."

Zanon resides in the Columbus, Ohio, suburb of Upper Arlington, a Tree City USA community, where he tends to his vegetable, herb, and perennial gardens. The longtime chair of the Green Committee at The Ohio State University Golf Club, he is currently a member of the Upper Arlington City Tree Commission. the American Horticultural Society, the Chadwick Arboretum, the Garden Writers Association, the Ohio Chapter International Society of Arboriculture, the Ohio Nursery & Landscape Association, the Ohio Turfgrass Foundation, and the Perennial Plant Association.

Photo courtesy of Jim Brown Photography, Columbus, Ohio